THE AMERICAN CIVIL WAR TRIVIA BOOK

Interesting American Civil War
Stories You Didn't Know

Trivia War Books Vol. 3

BY
BILL O'NEILL

DON'T FORGET YOUR FREE BOOKS

GET THEM FOR FREE ON
WWW.TRIVIABILL.COM

CONTENTS

INTRODUCTION

Some people say it's about states' rights. Some people say it's about owning slaves. Most people split the difference and say it's about a state's right to own slaves. Even a hundred and fifty years after its end, the Civil War remains one of the most relevant and most controversial events in American history. The North-versus-South tensions, the legacy of slavery, and the debates over state and federal power are still in the middle of practically every major American news story today.

But what really happened during the Civil War... and why? What are "states' rights," and why were they so controversial? How could anyone have supported slavery in the first place? Was the Civil War really the bloodiest war ever?

This book will guide you through the Civil War's slough of named battles and web of confusing politics. It will bring you up to speed on the debates that led to the war and the debates that happened afterward. The names Abraham Lincoln and Robert E.

Lee are probably familiar, but you'll find out what they did to get so famous. You'll also get to meet some characters who are a little bit lesser-known but who lived equally thrilling lives—from ten-year-old John Lincoln Clem to 54th Massachusetts leader Robert Gould Shaw.

With this book, you'll quickly become an expert in the daunting history of the Civil War, and you'll never again have to ask "What?" when someone brings up Chattanooga or Sherman's March. But even more importantly, with this background of knowledge about the Civil War, you'll be able to form more educated, critical opinions about what's going on in the United States today, because, as Robert Penn Warren said, you can learn a lot about a moment in American culture by how they talk about the Civil War. It's going to touch on some controversial issues—ones that are still relevant today—but, hopefully, with its help, you'll have an easier time understanding and navigating those issues for yourself.

The Civil War itself lasted just five years—from 1860 to 1865—five years in which over two hundred *thousand* people (civilians and soldiers alike) were killed. But to really understand what happened, we need to turn back the clock to the very first days of the plantation system in the South. Why were slaves so important? How could anyone have ever wanted to go die in a war to protect slavery when it's so obviously terrible? We'll also need to look forward at what happened after the Civil War was declared over. What exactly was Reconstruction, and why were people so upset about it? How did we go from fighting a war to end slavery to forbidding black people to use the same water fountains as white people? Is it okay now, in 2018, for someone to carry the Confederate flag?

You'll find the answers to these questions and dozens more in the book that's coming. It's divided into six quick-to-read chapters, each with fifteen stories about the chapter's main topic. These stories will give you an outline of events (so that you never have to look uneducated at a dinner party again), but they'll also give you the nitty-gritty details about daily life and introduce you to the colorful characters of the War. At the end of each chapter, there's a whole section of fun facts and trivia—did you know the can opener was invented during the Civil War?—and a few challenging questions to test your knowledge!

So get ready to find out...

Who said that slavery was "a positive good?"

Who was "the little woman who wrote the book that started this great War?"

Why would people who didn't own slaves bother going to war to protect slave-owners?

Why was the president of the Confederacy dressed in women's clothing?

And much, much more!

CHAPTER ONE

TROUBLE IN THE SOUTH

The American South faced a huge problem during the nineteenth century. For the last several hundred years, people in the Southern states, like the Carolinas and Georgia, had been enjoying a prosperous economy based on systems of huge farms. True, thousands of people were living in grinding poverty, but there was an upper class of people so rich that it's kind of mindboggling.

But as the century turned, things weren't looking so good for the rich. The real money, they were quickly realizing, wasn't in farming anymore. Northern states were making a whole lot more money by building factories and manufacturing goods. And more importantly, those Northern states—now that they weren't busy trying to eke out a living on substandard farmland—were looking down at the South and starting to judge the ways that they were making money. It wasn't looking good for those plantation owners.

Expectations

From the very first days of settlement in the United States, there was tension between the southern states and the northern states. People coming from Europe expected America to be more or less the same as their home countries in terms of climate. They thought it would be good farmland. And for the most part, they were right… in the south.

Southern states like Alabama, the Carolinas, and Georgia were great farmland where crops flourished. This made it easier for people who were coming to America with some money already in their pockets to buy huge swaths of land and set up massive mega-farms or plantations. They farmed easy-to-ship products like rice, and later, cotton.

The northern states like Pennsylvania, Massachusetts, and Connecticut had a bit of a different situation. These states were still pretty good farmland but nowhere near the level of the ones to the south. People could run great family farms, but it wasn't fertile enough for the hundred-acre plantations of the south. Northern states were more successful in industrial projects, like fish-curing and forestry.

Slaves in the South

These plantations that ran the economy in the South needed a lot of people. A *lot* of people. There were no huge motorized tractors or automatic fertilizer dispensers like today. If you wanted to run a farm that covered hundreds or even thousands of acres and still actually make money, well, you couldn't afford to just *pay* your workers! It was way cheaper to just *buy* people to do the work and then not pay them! Human rights? What are those?

Seriously, though, at a time before people had completely figured out the idea that owning other people was unacceptable, slavery made a lot of economic sense in the South. Without it, those states definitely would not have been able to support their massive plantation systems, and the economy of the South—where industrialization was still a long way off—would have collapsed.

Did Everyone in the South Own Slaves?

The answer to that one is a big no! In fact, only about a third of the people in the South owned slaves. This makes sense when you think about it. After all, when people who own slaves are owning enormous tracts of land, many hundreds of acres, it stands to reason that there really can't be all that many of them. They just wouldn't fit!

About one-third of people in the South owned slaves, and of that number, a lot of them owned one or two, and they were "domestic" rather than "plantation" slaves. In other words, they helped around the house, cooking, cleaning, or helping raise children, rather than on a plantation.

Why would people who didn't own plantations own slaves? It was because the American South was a society that put an enormously high value on owning slaves. They were seen as massive status symbols, and the only way to *be* anyone in the Southern states was to own them. Therefore, even people who didn't really have any need for free labor (and who didn't really have the means to buy it in the first place) either bought slaves or aspired to buy them.

The majority of slaves were owned by a small group of extremely rich families known as the "planter aristocracy," the equivalent of the "one percent" today. These were the people who have been immortalized in movies about the South and owned the massive plantations, wore white suits and ball gowns, and lounged around drinking lemonade while their slaves broke their backs to rake in the money to support their lavish lifestyle.

The Cotton Gin

Societies have owned slaves since ancient history, but life as a slave in the American South before the Civil

War was especially nasty because of the kind of work that they were expected to do. The work that slaves in the South did might include domestic labor, like cooking and cleaning, but most of the time, they were expected to work from dawn until dusk on plantations farming rice, corn, and especially cotton.

In 1793, a man named Eli Whitney had invented a machine called a cotton gin that prepared cotton fiber to be spun into thread and woven into fabric. The cotton gin made producing cotton much easier and led to a huge demand for cotton fabric. However, the first stage of the process—growing and picking the cotton—was as difficult as ever. For that reason, slave owners in the South (where cotton grew) bought more and more slaves to do more and more work picking cotton.

Daily Life for an American Slave

Considering how difficult the work was, you might think that slave owners would want slaves to be healthy, strong, and pretty well taken care of so that they would be as productive as possible. Unfortunately, you'd be wrong. Slave owners wanted to spend as little money as possible on their slaves, so they didn't bother paying very much for things like food, shelter, or even clothing. Slaves usually only got to eat bread or vegetables—not much protein considering how much physical labor they had to do. They were typically provided with new clothes about once a year and had to wear them no matter what labor they were doing. Houses were usually small shacks made of sticks—or log cabins if you were lucky—with dirt floors and nothing covering the windows.

Slaves were allowed to marry each other, even encouraged, since, legally, whoever owned the parents also owned any potential children. However, they had to ask permission, and the law wouldn't do anything to protect the marriage if the owner decided he wanted to sell off members of the family. Women were at constant risk of sexual violence and had no legal recourse for accusing their owners of rape since they were supposed to be their property. In fact, slaves had no way to legally prosecute their masters for anything, no matter how violently they were treated. It was even legal in some states for a white person to kill a slave if they were doing it as a "correction" or punishment for bad behavior.

Frederick Douglass

One of the things that people who supported slavery said—when they were trying to argue in favor of keeping their slaves around—was that slaves did not have the intellectual capacity to live on their own if they were free. This came from a very long tradition of black people being seen in Europe as intellectually inferior, one that still sometimes comes up today.

Abolitionists—people who opposed slavery—only had to point to Frederick Douglass to prove that argument wrong.

Frederick Douglass was born in Maryland to a slave mother, which automatically made him a slave too. When he was twelve years old, Frederick learned to read, first from his owner's wife and then from the white children who lived nearby. He became very passionate about reading, saying in one of his books that "knowledge is the pathway from slavery to freedom."

Among the things he read were several books and articles published by early abolitionists. Frederick started to develop a distinct sense of morality and feel that he had a right to freedom, just like anyone else ought to. When he was twenty years old, Frederick disguised himself as a sailor and escaped through Delaware with forged papers claiming that he was a free man. In less than a day, he arrived in Philadelphia, a notoriously anti-slavery city, where he was safe.

But Frederick's life story didn't end there. He wasn't satisfied just becoming educated and escaping from slavery. Frederick Douglass was committed to changing the world for the better and freeing everyone who was being kept under the cruel treatment of slavery. He became a preacher and connected with many other powerful abolitionists with whom he developed a powerful series of arguments against slavery.

In 1845, he published his bestselling autobiography, *Narrative of the Life of Frederick Douglass, an American Slave*. This book was so well written that some people who believed black people were innately inferior thought that a slave couldn't possibly have written it. But Frederick really had, and he went on to publish two more books about his life: *My Bondage and my Freedom* and *The Life and Times of Frederick Douglass*. His books became some of the most famous ones that were used to make arguments against slavery, and they opened many people's eyes to the horrors that slaves were forced to endure in the South.

The Underground Railroad

Not everyone could escape virtually single-handedly the way Frederick Douglass did. For many slaves, escape from even the cruelest owners was almost as perilous as staying. The Underground Railroad was a system set up by people who opposed slavery to try to get slaves out of the most dangerous situations and help them escape to freedom.

The Underground Railroad was neither a railroad nor underground. It was a series of houses equipped to hide slaves on the run. These houses were owned by abolitionists or sympathetic allies, often religious or community leaders. The houses had secret passages or hidden rooms built into them so that fugitive slaves could conceal themselves if any law enforcement officers seeking runaways came by. The owners of the houses could provide food, disguises, and information about where to move next on the route to safety.

Because even the Northern states where slavery was abolished had laws saying that it was illegal to harbor an escaped slave from a slave state, these trails of safe houses generally had to lead out of the country. Most of them went to Canada, some to Mexico, and some to the free areas of the Caribbean Islands where there were already large communities of former slaves. *Historica Canada* estimates that about 30,000 slaves escaped into Canada, and possibly over 100,000 worldwide.

Slavery Worldwide

But wait! you might say. Didn't other countries own slaves too? Weren't there slaves in the North? In Europe? What about in Canada? What about the huge plantations in the West Indies? What made the American South so different?

Yes, all those places had relied on slavery for a huge chunk of time. The slave plantations in the West Indies were even bigger and just as nasty as the ones in the American South, and slave labor wasn't exactly unheard of in Northern states, Europe, or Canada. However, starting in the late 1700s, more and more countries were starting to see slavery as unacceptable. People started to think of it as not just ethically questionable or "less than ideal," but actually as evil.

Bolstered by general negative opinion, the rest of the world saw a number of slave revolts and uprisings in the early 1800s. In 1831, over fifty thousand slaves in Jamaica (one of the biggest slave-driven colonies in the British Empire) led a revolution that contributed to Britain abolishing slavery two years later.

Since the British empire was pretty much the most powerful on earth at the time, and it basically controlled the oceans, they had a lot of power when it came to setting precedent for international law. If Britain said that slavery was out, then slavery was on its way out.

Slavery in the North

Let's be clear: people in the North *did* own slaves. A lot of people have the impression that slavery ended in the North right after the American Revolution, and that just isn't true. The process of slavery "going out" in the northern states took several decades, and a lot of the states kept slaves around right up until the Civil War started.

New England—the states of Maine, Vermont, and Massachusetts—got rid of slavery pretty quickly after the American Revolution. By the 1790s, none of those states had any slaves on the census. But they were in the minority. Other states, like Rhode Island and Pennsylvania, had relatively small slave populations that trickled off as the nineteenth century wore on, and by the time the Civil War started, they had been slave-free for a few decades. New York, on the other hand, had thousands and thousands of slaves, and the numbers didn't tank until 1827, when all slaves born before 1799 (i.e. almost all of them) were granted freedom.

Different states put different plans in place to try to slowly phase out slavery, like laws saying that you couldn't be *born* a slave just because your parents were slaves, and laws limiting the importation of slaves from other states or colonies. Although some of the plans were very slow-moving, they all pointed in the same direction. Slavery was not going to be the law of the land anymore.

The South Gets Defensive

So, people all over the world were telling the Southern states that they needed to figure out a new way to manage their economy. The old way, people said, was not only impractical for a new industrialized world, but it was also morally and ethically wrong, and people who profited from it were morally and ethically wrong.

Perhaps unsurprisingly, this did not sit well with the people who were profiting from it. They objected to the idea that they were doing something wrong. As soon as morality entered the picture, neither North nor South was going to be able to have a productive discussion about the possibility of ending slavery, because both sides were so sure that they were morally right, and the other side was morally wrong.

Before long, people in the South were developing an entirely new way of looking at slavery—not as a necessary evil, a way of keeping an economy afloat, but as a positive good that benefited both slave owners and the slaves themselves.

Slavery as a Positive Good

It may be hard to believe that anyone ever thought that being enslaved could be *good* for someone, but it happened. And the best example of what this line of thought looked like was when South Carolina politician named John C. Calhoun made a speech called "The Positive Good of Slavery" to the United States Senate.

For decades, people in the South had been making lots of different arguments in favour of slavery: it was the only way the Southern economy could function, it was necessary to provide the North with the raw materials that were funding their economy, and the numbers of slaves were so great that they couldn't be freed all at once without total political upheaval. In other words, most of these people were arguing that slavery was a necessary evil.

Calhoun had a different attitude. He made the bold argument that slavery was actually a *good* thing.

First, he told the Senate that he was not going to make any compromises with them. He argued that any concessions that the South made were going to be used against them by the more powerful North. Right from the beginning, he set himself up as a hard-nosed, unbending politician. When he said, "Abolition and the Union cannot coexist," people knew that he wasn't going to back down from that.

But that brusque opening was nothing compared to the tactic he took next.

Never before has the black race of Central Africa, from the dawn of history to the present day, attained a condition so civilized and so improved, not only physically but morally and intellectually. It came among us in a low, degraded, and savage condition, and in the course of a few generations, it has grown up under the fostering care of our institutions, reviled as they have been, to its present comparatively civilized condition. This, with the rapid increase of numbers, is conclusive proof of the happiness of the race in spite of all the exaggerated tales to the contrary.

In other words, Calhoun makes the jaw-dropping argument that black people—who he claims came to the United States "in a low, degraded, and savage condition" — were actually *benefiting* from being slaves. He argued that their "comparatively civilized condition" was the direct result of the harsh discipline they were kept under when they were enslaved.

Obviously, Calhoun's grandiose argument and tenuous evidence didn't make much of an impact on people who already basically agreed that slavery was a bad idea. No abolitionist was going to be swayed by an argument like that. But a lot of people caught in the middle between being skeptical of slavery and not wanting too much political turmoil were all too happy to latch on to Calhoun's argument and stand by him in his claim that slavery was "a positive good."

States' Rights

So, people in the North were leaning on the South to start phasing out slavery, while people in the South were hearing sound bites about how slavery was a positive good. With this in mind, the argument became who gets to decide whether a state should have slaves or not?

From the very beginning, the United States put a heavy focus on individualism. The Declaration of Independence was against a strong centralized government and supported smaller state governments having the right to make their own decisions about their own affairs.

For many people in the South, the fact that the North was pressuring them to make legal changes went directly against the idea of states having individual rights over their own governance. The way they saw it, it was unfair of the Northern government to put so much pressure on them, when the issues of slavery, they argued, didn't even affect the North. Political leaders said that the North could make decisions about its own laws on slavery, but it couldn't force the South to make decisions about theirs.

"Poor White Trash"

There was another group of people in the South who didn't exactly benefit from the system of slavery but whose opinions on it still counted towards its popularity, and who continue, even into the twenty-first century, to be seen as the people who can mostly be blamed for racism in the United States. These people are the poverty-stricken white people living in the South—people who were for centuries unironically called in professional statements "poor white trash."

Life for the extremely poor in the South was not that much better than life for slaves. They had little political power, ground out a living by hunting or growing gardens in extremely poor land, and sometimes had to live on the lands of rich plantation owners, usually without the owners knowing. But there was one thing that made life a little better for them: they were white. And in the States, being white, even if you were also horrifyingly poor, made a lot of difference.

Many of these people supported slavery, but not because they reaped any actual benefits from it. In fact, they were actually suffering from slavery because it limited the job market. Who would want to pay a free person to do farm work when they could have a slave do it for free? Poor white Southerners' reason for supporting slavery was that it kept them from occupying the very lowest rung in society.

As long as slaves existed, the logic went, the slaves were at the lowest possible position. "White trash" was bad, but it wasn't as bad as slavery. If slaves were freed, then extremely poor white Southerners would become the new lowest class, or so they feared.

It's impossible to say how things would have panned out if the Southern states had phased out slavery slowly (rather than in a violent war), but tensions did run very high between white and black Southerners after the war, and many of the people inciting violence were not the rich planter aristocracy who had actually lost property when abolition came around. Even today, the stereotype that poor white Southerners are the most racist people in America remains.

Uncle Tom's Cabin

In 1852, a little novel written by a moderately successful author and mother of seven children set off a powder keg of anti-slavery emotions.

Harriet Beecher Stowe was a young woman from Connecticut whose religious education had mostly prepared her for a life as a devout wife and mother. However, all those years learning about morality had also given Harriet a strong sense of right and wrong that prompted her to join the abolitionist movement and do her part advocating against slavery. She and her husband were supporters of the Underground Railway, and they helped many fugitive slaves get out of the Southern states to safety in the North or in Canada. But when new laws were passed that put harsh punishments in place for anyone found helping a slave to escape, the Stowes had to try a new tactic.

In 1850, while attending communion, Harriet had a vision of a dying slave and was inspired to tell a story of a pious, virtuous slave who was forced to suffer under an unjust master. She wanted to show the world a personal side of slavery and get the reading public to actually empathize with slaves on a person-to-person level, rather than just thinking of them as theoretical figures.

The novel that Harriet wrote, *Uncle Tom's Cabin*,

became an instant bestseller. People were shocked and appalled by the graphic descriptions of slavery — the demeaning treatment, the cruelty, and the total lack of options for escape. It stirred people's emotions in a way that speaking theoretically about an idea like slavery just couldn't. It also showed how the effects of slavery could be felt all through society and that it was making people other than just the slaves suffer.

Harriet intended her book to be educational and to encourage people to rally against slavery. She had no idea how powerful it would end up being. Ten years after it was published, during the height of the war, she visited Abraham Lincoln in the White House, where he allegedly looked at her and said with a smile, "so this is the little woman who wrote the book that started this great war."

The 1860 Election

As so often happens, the divisive argument about slavery became the central issue in a presidential election. In 1860, Abraham Lincoln and the other Republican anti-slavery candidates scored a whopping 82% of the national votes—a landslide victory. However, most of their votes were concentrated in the North in states that were already phasing out slavery and wouldn't be affected much by any new anti-slavery legislation. In the South, it was a very different story.

People felt that they weren't being represented by the federal elections. They feared their voices weren't being heard and that if they went on, they were just setting themselves up for all the power to be taken away from them. In their struggle to justify slavery, enthusiastic Southern politicians created a whole narrative of oppression that somehow made them into the victims of a tyrannical state rather than slaves being the victims of a violent system.

Lincoln won the election, but before he could even be inaugurated, seven states had declared that they were not going to accept him as president. In fact, they didn't even want to be part of the United States anymore at all.

RANDOM FACTS

1. Before the cotton gin was introduced, it took one person about ten hours to prepare one pound of cotton for spinning. After it was introduced, a team of two people working it could produce about fifty pounds in the same amount of time.

2. "Abolitionist" literally means a person who supports ending or abolishing any institution. However, anti-slavery advocates adopted the term, and it is now synonymous with anti-slavery.

3. Some abolitionists were surprised, or even angry, that Frederick Douglass was willing to talk to slave owners and try to find common ground and compromise in their values. They asked him how he could possibly try to unite with people who believed in something so terrible. Douglass's response to that was, "I would unite with anybody to do right and with nobody to do wrong."

4. Frederick Douglass's friends were worried, after the publication of his books, that his old owner would try to kidnap him or force the government to give him back, so he made a trip to Ireland while the hype died down. That happened to be right at the beginning of the Irish potato famine,

and he had many conversations with Irish nationalists about what it was like living under oppressive tyrant governments.

5. Thomas Jefferson, third president of the United States, blamed the South's obsession with slavery at least in part on their weather. "For in a warm climate," he said, "no man will labor for himself who can make another labor for him."

6. *Uncle Tom's Cabin* inspired a lot of southern, pro-slavery writers to write rebuttals. These books were called "anti-Tom novels," and they tried to portray the "positive good" of slavery by telling stories of contented slaves treated by kindly masters. Needless to say, this genre has not stuck around.

7. *Uncle Tom's Cabin* was made into a stage musical just a few months after its publication.

8. Even though at the time *Uncle Tom's Cabin* was considered an incredibly progressive anti-slavery and anti-racist book, it's gotten a bad reputation in the last hundred years for being sentimental as well as being racist itself. That's not exactly surprising, given the time it was written, but many critics object to the portrayal of the title character, a slave named Uncle Tom, as overly passive and too kind to the white people who mistreat him. "Uncle Tom" became an insult

directed at black people who are seen as acting subserviently towards white people.

9. People who organized the movement of escaped slaves on the Underground Railroad were known as "conductors."

10. In order to maintain secrecy, almost no one on the Underground Railroad knew the whole route. They only knew how to transport slaves from one safe house to the next one on the route. They didn't know where the slaves came from or even where the end goal was. This prevented anyone from being able to expose the whole operation, either by mistake, out of malice, or under duress from the government.

11. One of the most famous of these conductors was Harriet Tubman, an escaped slave herself, who freed over seventy slaves in thirteen trips. She had an excellent ability to move in secrecy, and none of her "passengers" ever got caught. Once she got them to Canada, she also helped the freed former slaves to find work so that they could set themselves up for a good life.

12. The Ohio River marked the boundary between free and slave states. Slaves referred to it in code as the "River Jordan," using a Biblical reference to secretly communicate about the way to freedom.

13. Contrary to popular depiction, Abraham

Lincoln's beard was not always his trademark. He was clean-shaven when he gained office but allegedly decided to grow a beard after an eleven-year-old girl named Grace Bedell wrote a letter to him suggesting that he would look better with one.

14. Many abolitionists were not wild about the idea of sharing a country with a whole lot of freed slaves. They may have been against slavery, but they weren't always pro-equality.

15. One popular abolitionist solution for the issue of not wanting to share a country with freed slaves was the "colonization program." The idea of this program was to move freed slaves to a colony in Africa rather than keeping them in America. Thomas Jefferson, Andrew Jackson, and even Harriet Beecher Stowe all supported this idea.

16. There were strong political efforts to create colonization projects in Central America or in the British Honduras, but nothing significant ever came to fruition.

17. Lincoln was a supporter of colonization too. In fact, he supported it so much that halfway through the war, he brought five black politicians to the White House and told them that "it would be better for us both to be separated."

18. Lincoln also said, "I am not, nor have ever been in

favor of bringing about in any way the social and political equality of the white and black races." He became a little more pro-equality towards the end of his career, but he was still pretty staggeringly racist by modern standards.

19. On the bright side, Lincoln was the first American president to propose that women should be allowed to vote.

20. Many slaves who escaped the South were very passionate about education. One woman, named Susie King Taylor, later became one of the first black nurses in the United States during the war and taught soldiers how to read while she was tending to them.

Test Yourself – Questions and Answers

1. What is a cotton gin?

   a. A type of alcohol derived from the cotton plant
   b. A machine that efficiently prepared cotton for spinning
   c. A cheap cotton fabric used for clothing for slaves

2. Which of these states was the first to ban slavery?

   a. New York
   b. Pennsylvania
   c. Vermont

3. Who argued that slavery was "a positive good"?

   a. John C. Calhoun
   b. Abraham Lincoln
   c. Robert E. Lee

4. Who wrote *Uncle Tom's Cabin?*

   a. Frederick Douglass
   b. Harriet Beecher Stowe
   c. Susie King Taylor

5. What were people involved in the Underground Railroad called?

   a. Conductors
   b. Railroaders
   c. Abolitionists

Answers

1. b
2. c
3. a
4. b
5. a

CHAPTER TWO

THE SECESSION

Tensions were running high in the 1840s and '50s, and as the decades wore on and the South got more and more defensive about its position on slavery, more and more people were whispering that things had to change. Calhoun's passionate statement that "abolition and the Union cannot coexist" stopped sounding like a dramatic anti-abolition statement and started sounding like more of a statement against the Union. In 1860, the South put their collective foot down and said that they were no longer interested in being part of a United States that didn't allow them to make their own decisions about who could and could not own other people.

What is Secession?

"Secession" is a Latin word meaning "to withdraw from a larger entity." It refers to one small group choosing to leave a larger group, alliance, or political entity (like, say, a group of states that have been united... the United States, for example) for philosophical, moral, or economic reasons.

Depending on who you ask, there can be different reasons why secession can be the right option. Some philosophers state that any group should have the right to secede from any bigger group at any time without needing to justify themselves, in order to keep their own liberty and freedom of choice in place. Other philosophers would say that you better have a really good reason for seceding, since it can cause so much upheaval. The general consensus is usually that you should be able to offer some justification or reasoning for leaving an entity if that's what you want to do, but that it's not very appropriate for the larger entity to force the smaller one to stay if the smaller one has stated its wish to secede.

Often, secession is used as a kind of bargaining chip by unsatisfied groups or political entities: "do what we want or we're leaving." It's less common for a group to actually go through with it. But in 1860, seven slave states in the American South proved that they were deadly serious when they said they no longer wanted to be part of a Union that didn't let them own slaves.

Who Seceded?

The first states to say that they wanted out of the Union were the heavily slave-reliant states of Georgia and Louisiana. Alabama, Mississippi, Florida, Texas, and South Carolina were quick to jump on the bandwagon too, and interestingly, the order in which states voted for secession was directly proportional to the numbers of slaves in those states. Those seven states formed the original group of seceded states and named themselves the Confederate States of America, in contrast to the United States of America. The following spring, they were joined by the "Upper South" states of Virginia, Arkansas, Tennessee, and North Carolina.

All the states that seceded had slave-reliant economies, but not all slave-reliant economies seceded. Missouri and Kentucky were both pro-Confederate states, but neither of them ever officially seceded, and their governments remained part of the United States, although there were strong attempts by Confederate forces to take political power in those regions.

Most people were not eager for a war, Lincoln included. He even tried to assure the Southern states that he wasn't planning on abolishing slavery, saying, "I have no purpose, directly or indirectly, to interfere with the institution of slavery in the United States where it exists. I believe I have no lawful right to do so, and I have no inclination to do so." For all the South's worrying about states' rights, Lincoln was coming down hard on the side that states could make their own laws. But he could not appeal to or compromise with the Confederate leaders, and both sides were quickly making preparation for war.

Democrats and Republicans

A quick note before we get any farther: In the 1800s, "Democrats" and "Republicans" were political parties with totally different meanings than the ones that they have now. Today, we generally associate the Democrat Party with work on social issues, a more involved federal government, and generally more left-leaning politics, while we associate the Republican Party with more individualistic, less federal, and generally more right-leaning politics. This is completely opposite to the way things were during the Civil War.

The Democrats were a very long-standing political party. They were the direct descendants of the first presidents of the United States, but by the middle of the 1800s, they were most active in the South, and they were known for their support of agriculture and strong focus on states' rights. They were also *very* pro-slavery.

The reason they were pro-slavery is that, around 1854, all the former Democrats who had opposed slavery actually cut ties with the Democratic Party and formed their own party, which they called the Republicans.

Republicans were against slavery, and anyone against slavery voted with them. While the Democrats were interested in supporting agriculture, the Republicans were more focussed on supporting industry and gave the most benefits to business owners, professionals, and factory workers. Because, at the time, these projects needed a national bank and more of a centralized government, the Republican Party became known as the one that supported a stronger federal government.

Whose Fault was Secession?

According to the leaders in the South who led the secession, this was the result of the American federal government becoming too involved in their decision-making processes and was the only fair and constitutional way forward.

According to the Union leaders—that is, the federal leaders—on the other hand, secession was an act of rebellion. The federal government blamed individual rebels for stirring up anti-United States sentiment among innocent common people. They also saw it as a strong strategic move by rich slaveholders to try to make wanting to own slaves into a constitutional issue rather than a moral or philosophical problem. These slave owners were doing their best to get people who *wouldn't* benefit from continued slavery onto their side by directing attention away from the core issue and on to the federal government.

Whether you see it as a democratic (if morally problematic) political move or as a rebellion encouraged by a small handful of privileged people to maintain their power, there's no doubt that there were some charismatic leaders behind it.

Jefferson Davis

Jefferson Davis, the eventual president of the Confederacy, was born in the tiny border town of Fairview, Kentucky. He had been the leader of the Democratic Party in the United States Senate before the Southern states seceded from the Union. His family owned cotton plantations, and he himself owned a massive plantation with more than seventy slaves. In other words, he was the exact kind of person who supported secession.

Only he *didn't* support secession. Not at first. When discussions of secession came up in 1858, he argued against it, saying that it was much better for the entire United States to figure out a set of restrictions and protections on states' rights rather than some states just leaving. He also warned the Southern states that there was really no way that the North was going to let them secede peacefully, and it would lead to bloodshed on both sides. However, he did state then that he believed that states had the *right* to secede from the Union if that was what they really wanted to do. He just didn't think it was a good idea.

By 1861, he had changed his tune. Mississippi, the state he was governing at the time, seceded from the Union despite his warnings, and he decided that he was more faithful to his state of Mississippi than to the United States as a whole. Mississippi made him the General of the Army of Mississippi and then provisional president of the Confederate States, putting him in charge of overseeing the war efforts.

Abraham Lincoln, Part 1: His Childhood

Probably the most famous figure from the Civil War, Abraham Lincoln was elected as President of the United States just as the Confederate States were seceding. He is going to continue to be one of the biggest characters in the story of the Civil War, so let's take a little time to get to know him.

Lincoln was born in 1809, in a cabin in rural Kentucky, the same state as Jefferson Davis. The town of Hodgenville was on the western frontier, and Lincoln's family was doing the hard work of "breaking" the land for human habitation. Stories about Lincoln's childhood circulated widely, with many people saying that he was lazy because he spent all his time inside reading and writing rather than outside laboring. There wasn't much in the way of formal education in the Kentucky backwoods, but Lincoln was a wide reader.

In the 1830s, he got on board with the Whig Party, which was the precursor to the Republican Party, a socially conscious, left-leaning group that stood against the Democrat Party's platform of slavery and weak federal government. He entered the House of Representatives as a Whig in 1846, and one of his big projects in early politics was collaborating to write a bill to abolish slavery. He worked with an abolitionist congressman named Joshua R. Giddings, and the bill would have put slavery to a popular vote in the District of Colombia, but it didn't get the support to pass through. For the moment, Lincoln set aside the issue of slavery.

Abraham Lincoln, Part 2: Lincoln On Slavery

In the 1850s, Lincoln was working hard to get a conversation going between both sides of the slavery debate to try to come to some kind of conclusion or consensus. Lincoln made it very clear that he was against the *extension* of slavery into non-slave territory, but he was willing to work with states where slavery was a key part of the economy so that their economies didn't crash and burn.

In these early days, Lincoln's views on slavery were mixed. As we've already learned, he didn't exactly have a glowing view of black people. However, he thought that slavery was unconstitutional, since the Declaration of Independence *does* say that all men are created equal and have the right to life, liberty, and the pursuit of happiness, which slavery definitely stood in the way of.

The International Reaction

The Southern states made the decision to secede running under the assumption that they had a lot of international clout. After all, they were the world's main providers of cotton, one of the hottest commodities in the entirety of western Europe. If they weren't recognized, they weren't going to sell cotton to huge buyers like Britain and France, and also, if they were forced to reintegrate into the Union and get rid of their slaves, they wouldn't be able to support their massive cotton plantations on such small budgets. Overall, they figured that the rest of the world was too reliant on cotton to really stand up to them.

They were wrong. Britain and France—the two biggest superpowers in Europe for quite some time—had long since decided that slavery was out, so neither country was willing to show their support for a confederacy that was basically making an argument for slavery. Even if it meant potentially paying higher prices for cotton, no European superpower was about to go up against the recently-recognized United States in favor of what they saw as a pro-slavery rebellious faction.

The Confederate Soldiers' Early Moves

The first thing that the Confederate armies focussed on doing, once they had declared their independence from the United States, was to get rid of any federal powers that were hanging around in the South. They focussed on capturing forts and military installations that had belonged to the federal United States but that fell within "Confederated" territory.

The first real violent collision happened in 1861, when the Confederate army attacked Fort Sumter, a United States fort in South Carolina.

Fort Sumter was a powerful fortress on an island, overseeing the entrance to the Charleston Harbour, a useful strategic position. Knowing that they were being forced out of the state, United States military moved to Fort Sumter, abandoning most of their other forts in South Carolina. They were willing to lose their other posts as long as they could keep this one important strategic and symbolic fort.

But the Confederate army wasn't about to let that happen. Starting in January of 1861, and continuing for months, they laid siege to the fort. They constantly fired on it, making it impossible for anyone to enter or leave. Lincoln tried to send supplies by ship to the soldiers trapped inside, but the Confederate government refused to allow them in unless the fort was immediately evacuated and handed over to the Confederates.

On April 13th, after 34 solid hours of gunfire, the United States surrendered Fort Sumter to the Confederacy. They were outnumbered, the Confederates had far more weapons and could move more freely, and it just didn't seem worth the blood. However, the surrender at Fort Sumter bolstered the Confederates' confidence and encouraged them to continue moving in the direction of open warfare.

Expansionism

From the beginning of the 1800s to the beginning of the Civil War, the United States had been steadily acquiring more territory, and by the time the war hit, almost all of what is now the United States was either a state or a territory. Territories weren't a huge problem. The populations of white settlers were so low in them that the issue of slavery didn't come up, and they didn't have to have a voice on the federal stage. But as more territories became states, those states' opinions about slavery (and other issues that were causing division between North and South, like industrialization, or the right to secede) had to be listened to.

Because of this, the United States' project to expand across the continent actually led to more destruction and violence as new states became new theatres for North-versus-South tensions to break into outright conflict.

Bleeding Kansas

A little further north, the newly created state of Kansas was suffering a series of violent confrontations between abolitionists and pro-slavery advocates. Kansas was caught in a controversy about whether it should allow slavery or not, and the federal government had unknowingly poured gas on the fire in 1854, when they passed the Kansas-Nebraska Act, which said that decisions in Kansas would be made by popular sovereignty—that is, by popular vote, counted across the settlers in the territory.

Since the decision would be made by popular vote, thousands of people flooded into Kansas to settle for the sole purpose of trying to sway the vote in their direction. Pro-slavery people from Missouri poured in from the South, while anti-slavery New Englanders poured in from the North, each with their own clear agenda: to swing the elections in their favor.

When you're playing a numbers game like the settlers of Kansas were, it wasn't enough to just bring people with your political opinions into the country. People also felt the pressing need to get rid of people who disagreed with them. In 1855, a pro-slavery settler shot an anti-slavery settler and sparked a run of open violence between the two factions. They burned and ransacked each others' homes and businesses, and devolving into street brawls and gunfights.

There was so much violence over this issue that Kansas became known as a hotbed of crime and gained the nickname "Bleeding Kansas." Guerilla warfare continued in the area into the beginning of the official Civil War. Kansas never joined the Confederacy, but it had enough violence to stand alongside the bloodiest southern battlegrounds.

Texas

To the north, Kansas was bleeding. To the south, the similarly new state of Texas was also posing problems. Texas had been an independent republic for nine years before it was made part of the United States, and before that, it had been part of Mexico.

The Mexican government had tried to outlaw slavery while Texas was a part of Mexico, but that had just led to outrage and violence all across the province. In fact, Mexico's attempt to outlaw slavery in Texas was part of the reason that it eventually declared its independence and later became incorporated into the United States, with the understanding that it would get to keep its slaves.

Texas was a huge territory compared to many other states, and it held a *lot* of slaves. Like Kansas, the pro-slavery and anti-slavery factions were constantly fighting, both in politics and in the streets. Texas had very little police force and was known for being lawless, the quintessential "wild west." The brawls that broke out between pro- and anti-slavery factions in Texas were particularly nasty, as slaveholders, abolitionists, western expansionists, and pro-Mexico advocates clashed, with nothing to stop them from straight-up murdering each other in the streets.

The Eastern Theatre

As fighting progressed, the major conflicts congealed into three groupings of operations: The Eastern Theatre, the Lower Seaboard Theatre, and the Western Theatre.

The Eastern Theatre included all the fighting that was going on in Virginia, Maryland, Pennsylvania, and North Carolina. It was where the infamous Robert E. Lee did most of his campaigns and where the famous battle of Gettysburg took place. In fact, almost all the really famous campaigns took place in the Eastern Theatre, not just because those campaigns were strategically important (although many were) or unusually bloody (although many were), but also because those battles took place in close proximity to large cities, where many people were around both to witness and be caught in the crossfire. The areas of the Lower Seaboard Theatre and the Western Theatre were much less densely populated, so far fewer people were there to immortalize the battles.

The Confederate army had a serious advantage in the Eastern Theatre, because, for the most part, they were defending territory that they already had control of. The rivers that ran from west to east across this territory were barriers that the Union army had to cross, while the Confederates, who were much more familiar with the terrain, could lie in wait. Since the Confederacy was operating with a much smaller army, they were happy to have the landscape on their side this way.

The Lower Seaboard Theatre

The Lower Seaboard Theatre was the one area of the Civil War that involved fighting by water. The naval efforts of the Civil War aren't nearly as well remembered as the land battles, but they were no less important.

Since a lot of the major Southern cities were accessible by water and got a lot of supplies transported by water, taking control of port cities would give the Union forces a huge advantage over the Confederate forces. Throughout the entire war, the Union was struggling to both stop the flow of supplies getting into port cities in the South and also capture those cities so they could have the strategic advantage of being on both land and water. Cities like Carolina and forts like Fort Pulaski in Georgia were constant targets of attacks from the Union forces as they tried to take strategic control over the South.

The Western Theatre

The Western Theatre encompassed all the fighting that was happening in Alabama, Georgia, Florida, Mississippi, Kentucky, Tennessee, and Louisiana, as well as a lot of what was happening in the Carolinas. The Mississippi River usually marks the cut-off point for what counts as "Eastern Theatre" and "Western Theatre," with whatever happens to the east counting as the Eastern Theatre and whatever happens to the west counting as the Western Theatre.

The Union military was very interested in campaigns that took them through the Western Theatre, because it took them right into the big agricultural areas of the South. These were poorly protected, spread-out areas that were hard to defend, which made it easy for the Union armies to take control of them. Most railways didn't cross through this area, so the Confederate army had to send soldiers on foot or by horse if they wanted to get protection here, and there was nothing much in the way of fortifications that they could rely on for protection. While there weren't as many huge and well-remembered battles in the Western Theatre as there were in the Eastern Theatre, this area was hugely important from a strategic point of view and was probably the only reason that the Union actually ended up having an advantage over the Confederacy at all.

RANDOM FACTS

1. In 1860, both Mississippi and South Carolina had more slaves than free people.

2. No soldiers were actually killed in the Battle of Fort Sumter.

3. On May 24, 1855, as part of the Bleeding Kansas crisis, a radical anti-slavery leader named John Brown led supporters into a pro-slavery camp where they gorily killed five supporters of slavery by hacking them into pieces with swords.

4. John Brown was executed on the order of Henry A. Wise, governor of Virginia. His execution was controversial. Even though he was an undisputed murderer, he was also seen by many as a martyr for the cause of abolition. After all, he was far from the only one killing in Bleeding Kansas.

5. John Brown reached such status as a martyr and folk hero among abolitionists that a folk song called "John Brown's Body" became a popular tune among the soldiers.

6. The tune was *so* popular that a poet named Julia Ward Howe, uncomfortable with the irreverent lyrics ("John Brown's body lies a-mouldering in the grave; his soul is marching on!... They will

hang Jeff Davis to a tree/as they march along!") wrote a new set of words to it… under the title "The Battle Hymn of the Republic." She replaced the lines about John Brown's mouldering body and Jefferson Davis's imminent hanging with "Mine eyes have seen the glory of the coming of the Lord; He is trampling out the vintage where the grapes of wrath are stored; He hath loosed the fateful lightning of His terrible swift sword; His truth is marching on."

7. Much like Jefferson Davis, Robert E. Lee, one of the most famous (and infamous) Confederate leaders, actually opposed secession. He also opposed slavery. He disagreed with the Confederacy's goals and methods, but he led the Confederate army out of loyalty to his home state of Virginia.

8. It wasn't until the 1940s that the Democratic Party started to develop its current reputation for being progressive on civil rights issues. Until then, the Democratic Party was still clinging to slavery and tended to be pretty explicitly racist.

9. When the Southern states seceded from the Union and started putting together an army, knowing they were going to have to fight the better-equipped North, they asked for all the volunteers they could get. Their army was still much smaller than the Union army.

10. The youngest person to serve in the Civil War was a boy named John Lincoln Clem, who was a drummer boy for the Union army at the age of only ten. He had first attempted to join an infantry but was rejected for being, you know, ten. After a few years as a drummer boy, however, he was promoted to sergeant for his bravery in battle.

11. Perhaps unsurprisingly, John Clem was the last veteran of the Civil War to remain on duty in the United States Armed Forces, all the way up to 1915.

12. Abraham Lincoln and Jefferson Davis were born only 100 miles apart.

13. Lincoln was the first United States president to not be born within the original thirteen colonies of the United States.

14. Lincoln is still the only American president who was born in Kentucky (unless you count Davis, of course).

15. Contemporary accounts suggest that both Lincoln and Davis suffered from clinical depression.

16. During the war, attempts from slaves to escape the South rose astronomically, from an estimated average of about 5,000 per year to over 5,000 per month.

17. Black men (both born free and escaped slaves) were extremely eager to enlist in the Union army for obvious reasons, but a 1792 law technically prevented them from serving, and Lincoln was concerned that repealing that law would cause border states to secede. Let's just say that there was a lot of anxiety about what might happen if ex-slaves were allowed to have guns and march through slave territory.

18. In 1862, black men were finally allowed to enlist in the Union army.

19. Black people did serve in the Confederate army, starting from the beginning—as a slave labor force. They were brought along to serve their owners and to replace them on the lines if they were killed.

20. In 1865, the Confederate government passed legislation saying any black person who enlisted in the Confederate army with the consent of their owners would be freed. Much too little, much too late, less than fifty black people in the South even bothered enlisting under this new legislation.

Test Yourself – Questions and Answers

1. When was Abraham Lincoln born?

   a. 1799
   b. 1809
   c. 1812

2. Who wrote the lyrics to "Battle Hymn of the Republic"?

   a. Harriet Beecher Stowe
   b. Julia Ward Howe
   c. John Clem

3. Which party was specifically against slavery?

   a. The Democrats
   b. The Whigs
   c. The Republicans

4. Which of these states did not secede from the Union?

   a. Texas
   b. Florida
   c. Kentucky

5. What was "Bleeding Kansas"?

   a. A name for the series of outbreaks of violence over slavery and secession in Kansas
   b. A reference to sentimental "bleeding heart" politics in Kansas
   c. A type of red fungus affecting crops in Kansas

Answers

1. b
2. b
3. c
4. c
5. a

CHAPTER THREE

THE BLOODIEST WAR
IN AMERICAN HISTORY

With 372 named battles and hundreds of skirmishes and side-conflicts, the Civil War frequently gets referred to as the bloodiest war in American history or the American war with the most casualties. While we're going to spend a minute thinking about that claim, there's no doubt that this was a war that caused unprecedented destruction to the United States. In this chapter, we're going to look at some of the biggest battles, the most important campaigns, and a few characters who can give us a little hint as to what life was like for a Civil War soldier.

Was the Civil War the Bloodiest War in American History?

The statistic gets pulled out all the time: The Civil War was the bloodiest war in American history, the war with the most casualties. Is that true?

Well, it *really* depends on how you look at the facts.

In terms of military casualties, about 215,000 soldiers were killed. This number is pretty massive considering that the number of American soldiers killed in World War II was around 291,500 — barely any bigger. But it's also a pretty misleading number, because unlike World War II, *all* the soldiers on *both sides* of the Civil War were American. The total number of soldiers killed in World War Two was more like 21 to 25 million, blowing the Civil War casualties out of the water. And World War One, the Vietnam War, and the Korean War (all of which the US fought in) also had *enormous* numbers of casualties, most of whom just didn't happen to be American.

So, yes, the most Americans were killed in the Civil War. If your metric for "bloodiest war in American history" is "most American citizens killed," then it's pretty much neck-and-neck with World War Two (just below it in military casualties, above it in civilian casualties). But it's hard to say if that's really a good metric.

It might be more intellectually honest to count the number of Union soldiers who died in the war, since they were the ones who actually self-identified with the United States, and that gives you the still pretty staggering number of 140,400 dead in combat. Not even close to the World War Two number, but it pretty much dwarfs every other conflict. And that's not taking into account civilian deaths, which bump the Civil War number *way* up, again because it was all taking place on American soil and everyone killed was an American. The US's big wars have otherwise taken place mostly on other people's ground.

Whatever way you slice it, though, it's hard to argue that the Civil War wasn't a pretty huge shock to the system. It was by far the bloodiest war Americans had fought in *up to that point*. And it was the setting for dozens of battles and military campaigns that are still remembered today.

The Anaconda Plan

The Anaconda Plan, proposed by the Union General in Chief Winfield Scott, was one of the first major strategies that the Union came up with when they were trying to limit the Confederacy's power early in the war. It was also the biggest campaign in the Lower Seaboard Theatre of the war. In fact, it was focussed almost entirely on the Union's power on the water.

The idea of the Anaconda plan was to send ships down the East Coast of the United States and block the ports in the South so that Confederate troops couldn't send for help or supplies from outside the continent. Then, the Union would send ships up the Mississippi River, cutting the western parts of the

Confederacy off from the eastern parts. They would fill the Mississippi River with Union soldiers, who could then cut off any communication—much less travel—that Confederates planned on moving around their territory.

Unfortunately for Scott and the Union, the United States Navy didn't have the power to pull off the Anaconda Plan in one fell swoop like Scott had in mind. Instead, they poured resources into it for years, and it continued for the entire duration of the war. But you couldn't quite call it unsuccessful. The division between the east and west parts of the Confederacy was one of the main reasons that it weakened over time and was eventually ready to be taken by the Union.

The Battle of Hampton Roads

The Battle of Hampton Roads was a naval battle at the beginning of March in 1862. It's sometimes called the Battle of the *Monitor* and *Merrimack*, the Battle of the *Monitor* and *Virginia*, or simply the Battle of Ironclads.

Union ships had put up a blockade Hampton Roads, a harbor in Virginia, trying to prevent Confederate ships from moving through it for strategic reasons or trade ships moving through it to bring supplies into the Southern states. The Battle of Hampton Roads was the Confederacy's attempt to break through the blockade using their newest and most powerful type of ships.

It was one of the few really dramatic naval battles of the Civil War, as two ironclad warships—a kind of warship that had never been used against each other in combat before—faced off in the Chesapeake Bay. A group of old-fashioned wooden ships entered the battle alongside the Confederate ship *Virginia* and the Union ship *Monitor*, but they soon fell victim to the superior weaponry of the ironclad ships. The battle itself was inconclusive; both sides dealt and received damage. The Confederate ships did more damage to the Union ships than the Union ships did to the Confederate ships, but the Confederate ships also failed their main objective of breaking down the blockade.

But no one cared very much about who won and who lost. The point was that the world had now seen what ironclad ships could do on the water. Naval powers around the world were shaken by the power of the two ships in battle. Britain and France both totally stopped producing conventional wooden ships after they saw what ironclad ships could do at this battle.

The Battle of Shiloh

At the beginning of April 1862, Union Major General Ulysses S. Grant got a surprise attack from the

Confederate Army of Mississippi. The Confederates ambushed the camp during the day and made huge hits against the Union soldiers, but their leader General Albert Sidney Johnston sustained serious injuries during the fighting and called off the attack for the night. While the Confederate army was recovering, Grant called in reinforcements. By the next morning, he had the manpower to repel the Confederate forces, killed almost as many Confederates as the Confederates had killed Unions the previous day, and made the battle into a Union victory.

Unfortunately for Grant, even though he successfully turned the whole battle around, the news cycle was not on his side. Newspaper reports wrote that Grant was unprepared, possibly even inebriated at the time of the battle, and that the enormous body count was his fault. Grant wrote in his memoirs that:

> The Battle of Shiloh, or Pittsburg landing, has been perhaps less understood, or, to state the case more accurately, more persistently misunderstood, than any other engagement between National and Confederate troops during the entire rebellion. Correct reports of the battle have been published... but all of these appeared long subsequent to the close of the rebellion and after public opinion had been most erroneously formed.

The Capture of New Orleans

At the end of April in 1862, the Union army captured the wealthy and strategically important city of New Orleans as part of the Anaconda plan. This was one of the most significant pieces of territory they could capture, because New Orleans sits right at the mouth of the Mississippi River. If the Union had control over New Orleans, they would have control over the entire Mississippi.

The Confederate defenses at New Orleans were ready for a land attack. Almost all their guns pointed towards the land where soldiers might march up towards the city. But Officer David G. Farragut of the Union wasn't attacking by land. He took a fleet up the Mississippi River and broke through New Orleans's water defenses—easily.

It wasn't just that New Orleans was poorly defended. Union ships on the water also had a huge tactical advantage. As you might remember from 2005, when Hurricane Katrina decimated present-day New Orleans, the city is essentially a bowl protected by levees that keep out high water. Well, the Union ships were up on that high water and threatening to break down the levees. They had a clear shot to fire on anything within the city, and if the Confederates even thought about returning fire, it would have been easy for the Union Navy to blast a hole in a levee and have the whole city underwater within a day.

The Battles of Bull Run

The First Battle of Bull Run was the first real battle of the Civil War—the first one fought on land, with soldiers, where people died. It was also not a good showing for the Union soldiers. The Union Army was still in a state of confusion, not ready for a fight. After all, this was the first real time they'd been called upon to do anything. There were about 18,000 people, mostly new recruits, on both sides, and the leaders didn't know what they were doing any better than the foot soldiers did. By the time the Union soldiers had even gotten into position, Confederate reinforcements had arrived, skewing the numbers and the power. The Union army retreated, disorganized and shaken, but the Confederates weren't doing much better. Everyone was thrown off by how serious the fighting was.

The First Battle of Bull Run was also the first showing of the infamous Stonewall Brigade, led by the even more infamous Thomas "Stonewall" Jackson. These were a Virginian Confederate troop known for their total unwillingness to back down under any circumstances. They got their name because the Union forces saw them like a stone wall that couldn't be broken down.

The Second Battle of Bull Run was more than a year later, and, if possible, went even worse for the Union.

This time, the Confederate Army had a clear focus and was under the leadership of Robert E. Lee, who had a lot more experience than any of the commanders of the First Battle of Bull Run. The scale was orders of magnitude bigger than the First Battle of Bull Run, with almost 80,000 soldiers on the Union side and 50,000 on the Confederate side. Stonewall Jackson was also there and ended up being a shocking danger to the Union army, not because of what he did but because of what the Union Major General John Pope planned to do to him. Partway through the battle, Pope became convinced that he had Jackson trapped and concentrated all his effort on taking down the Confederate leader—while the Confederates led a surprise counterattack that decimated the Union forces. Over 16,000 soldiers in the Union army were killed, wounded, or captured, and just around 9,000 Confederates were.

The Battle of Antietam

The Battle of Antietam in September 1862 became the first land battle of the Eastern Theatre to take place in Union territory. Robert E. Lee's Northern Virginia Army had moved into Maryland with the goal of getting fresh supplies to the Confederate armies while also continuing into Northern territory.

McClellan, the Union Major General, was unwilling to send his entire army against Lee's, even though he had plenty of forces at hand. The terrain was difficult to communicate across, and the commanders who were in charge of individual groups of soldiers had trouble knowing what their own men were doing, much less the men in other corps. Even though McClellan had almost twice as many men as Lee, they were uncoordinated and didn't inflict as much damage as anticipated.

Nevertheless, the Battle of Antietam did stop Lee from advancing into Maryland and ultimately prevented Lee from continuing with his campaign to capture Maryland for Confederate strategic purposes. Although McClellan was dismissed shortly afterwards by Lincoln as a poor military leader, the battle did have a good impact on the North's confidence, while having Maryland captured by the Confederates would almost certainly have decimated their morale.

The Battle of Gettysburg

If there's just one battle from the American Civil War that you know about, it's probably the Battle of Gettysburg. This was fought from July 1st to July 3rd in 1863, in the town of Gettysburg in Pennsylvania. The battle had the most casualties of any battle in the entire Civil War, with over 23,000 Union soldiers and between 23,000 and 28,000 Confederate soldiers, killed, captured, or wounded. Upwards of 200,000 soldiers were present for the battle.

The Battle of Gettysburg was the sharp stop to Confederate General Robert E. Lee's attempt to invade the North. He and his Army of Northern Virginia had been building up steam with victory after victory against Union forces in the South. In the height of summer, he was ready to move into undisputed Northern territory in Pennsylvania.

Lee's forces paused at Gettysburg to try to engage and conquer the Union army. The town was defended by Union forces, which Lee was confident he could take out. On the first day, he attacked the city, forcing the Union defenses into the hills for protection.

In the second day of the battle, the armies fought on the battlefield with both sides suffering enormous losses. But the Union held their position and were not conquered.

On the third day, things got worse for the Confederates. Lee led a charge of 12,500 soldiers against the Union lines, confident that the sheer numbers would overwhelm the Union forces. But he was wrong. The Union forces gunned them down with superior weapons, and almost the entire charge of Confederate soldiers was killed. With a loss that great, Lee had no option but to retreat. This was one of the greatest defeats of Confederate forces and is generally understood as the turning point of the war.

The Gettysburg Address

In the fall after the Battle of Gettysburg, a dedication ceremony for a cemetery honoring Union soldiers was held in Gettysburg, and Abraham Lincoln was invited to give a speech. It was a short speech, coming late in a programme of big-name speakers, but Lincoln's solemn words have gone down in history as one of the best speeches ever given for his thoughtful references to the Declaration of Independence, and his plea for peace and a resolution to the gory war.

He said:

> Four score and seven years ago, our fathers brought forth on this continent a new nation, conceived in Liberty and dedicated to the proposition that all men are created equal.

> Now we are engaged in a great civil war, testing whether that nation, or any nation so conceived and so dedicated, can long endure. We are met on a great battle-field of that war. We have come to dedicate a portion of that field, as a final resting place for those who here gave their lives that that nation might live. It is altogether fitting and proper that we should do this.

> But, in a larger sense, we cannot dedicate—we cannot consecrate—we cannot hallow—this ground. The brave men, living and dead, who struggled here, have consecrated it, far above our

poor power to add or detract. The world will little note, nor long remember what we say here, but it can never forget what they did here. It is for us the living, rather, to be dedicated here to the unfinished work which they who fought here have thus far so nobly advanced. It is rather for us to be here dedicated to the great task remaining before us—that from these honored dead we take increased devotion to that cause for which they gave the last full measure of devotion— that we here highly resolve that these dead shall not have died in vain—that this nation, under God, shall have a new birth of freedom—and that government of the people, by the people, for the people, shall not perish from the earth.

The Chattanooga Campaign

Another one of Ulysses S. Grant's major projects was the Chattanooga Campaign, a series of maneuvers to capture the strategically important railway city of Chattanooga in Tennessee. Chattanooga was the home of one of the biggest railway stations in the South, and whomever had control over that city had the ability to travel freely into the Confederate heartland. Supplies, soldiers, and civilians all travelled through Chattanooga, both going into and getting out of the South.

The Union wanted to have control of that. If they

occupied Chattanooga, they could take the railroads right into the South and get to strategic locations and Confederate bases much faster. At the same time, they would be able to cut off Confederate soldiers from getting supplies by rail, causing a shortage of ammunition and hopefully hastening a surrender.

Grant opened up a supply line called the "Cracker Line" that could feed Union forces in the area and then laid siege to Chattanooga, struggling to take control of the high ground around the city while also not letting any trains pass through.

The Battle of Chickamauga

The Chickamauga Campaign was a series of battles in the fall of 1863, when the Union commander William S. Rosecrans was trying to push the Confederates out of Tennessee and Georgia. Rosecrans's army had been hugely successful in a series of battles in Middle Tennessee, and their next move was to capture Chattanooga. Rosecrans faced off with an army under Confederate General Braxton Bragg, who was forced out of Chattanooga but determined to take it back.

On the morning of September 19, as the two armies were fighting, Rosecrans was informed that there was a gap in his line. He quickly sent a group of soldiers to plug it, but doing so turned out to be the exact wrong thing to do. There was no gap, but he created one by sending soldiers away. James

Longstreet, a Confederate General, sent his army through the gap, cutting Rosecrans and a huge chunk of his army off from the rest of it.

Fortunately, the rest of the Union army stepped up to the task and formed a new defense, preventing the Confederates from advancing any further. Although the Confederates had technically won the battle, because they forced Rosecrans off the battlefield, they did not regain control of Chattanooga, and the damage that they suffered in casualties was crushing.

Trans-Mississippi Guerrilla Warfare

The Mississippi River was a huge focal point for conflicts in the Civil War, so much so that it's sometimes referred to as the "Trans-Mississippi Theatre." This was the area in which the most guerrilla fighting was taking place.

The term "guerrilla warfare" was coined in the 1700s, based on the Spanish word *guerrilla*, meaning "little war." Guerrilla warfare is an alternative to traditional warfare of the sort practiced by most armies during the Civil War, which generally involves the newest technology, large numbers of soldiers in uniform, and battlefield locations—wide open spaces where people can see an attack coming and respond in a well-organized manner. In traditional warfare, success depends on the skill, numbers, and technology of one army being greater than that of the other.

On the other hand, guerrilla warfare relies on small groups of people—often locals rather than imported armies—who are able to move quickly and easily, especially through difficult terrain like the wildlands bordering the Mississippi River. The ability to move quickly gives guerrillas an advantage when they are dealing with larger armies in unfamiliar territory. Guerrilla units usually disguise themselves as civilians and hide in their home territory, seeking out small groups of enemy soldiers rather than attacking a full-sized troop. They move in small groups, rather than huge armies, which makes finding cover much easier for guerrillas than for traditional soldiers.

Along the Mississippi, Confederate guerrilla troops hid in the backwoods or the villages. These Confederate gangs were called "bushwhackers." Many of them attacked Union troops that were using the river for transportation, but many more attacked other locals who had Union sympathies. This was especially true in the state of Missouri, which was officially part of the Union but which harbored very strong Confederate sympathies.

Historians estimate that the scale of the guerrilla warfare along the Mississippi was much larger than was realized at the time. Some estimates suggest that the state's population fell by one-third when taking into account both the people killed and those forced to relocate out of the state for safety from the guerrilla forces. In the Lawrence massacre in 1863, a Confederate guerrilla group destroyed the entire abolitionist town of Lawrence and killed over a hundred and fifty civilians living there.

The Overland Campaign

The Overland Campaign was a series of battles led by our old friend Ulysses S. Grant over Virginia in May and June of 1864. It was one of the biggest, bloodiest campaigns of the Eastern Theatre. By the middle of 1864, both Union and Confederate armies were depleted and desperate to bring the war to a decisive close.

Grant's goal was to defeat Robert E. Lee's army and capture Richmond, Virginia, which was the capital of the Confederate States.

To do that, first, he had to stop reinforcements from reaching Lee's army in order to keep it weaker than the Union armies were. To do this, Grant cut the rail lines that ran between Richmond, Virginia, and Petersburg, Virginia. This interrupted the flow of both men and supplies.

Then, the Union army put pressure on Lee to come out into battle. The goal was to force him to fight with a depleted force, making him into an easy target.

The battles between the desperate undersupplied Confederate forces and the equally desperate Union forces were bloody. The Battle of Spotsylvania Court House, where Grant brought his troops south to cut off the Confederate Army of North Virginia from reaching Richmond, had over 30,000 casualties, including nearly three thousand Union soldiers dead and over thirteen thousand wounded.

Sherman's March to the Sea

Sherman's March to the Sea remains one of the most controversial acts of the Union army. It's hardly controversial to say that the Confederate army did terrible things (like fighting an entire war to preserve slavery), but it's a little touchier to talk about the bad things that the Union army did. But it was wartime, and as in so many wars, there were bad guys but no good guys.

Sherman's March to the Sea, also known as the Savannah Campaign, was a campaign by Union Major General William Tecumseh Sherman. He marched his troops from the city of Atlanta (which he had captured) to the port of Savannah (which he then captured), but it wasn't just a matter of capturing major strategic cities or fighting Confederate soldiers. He also dealt serious damage to the people living in the area between Atlanta and Savannah. The goal of the campaign was to disrupt the Confederate economy and destroy their transportation networks. This was pretty much an impossible goal to achieve without doing some damage to civilians.

Sherman's forces attacked industry, infrastructure, telegraph poles, railroads, and private property. They also freed slaves along the way, using their help to find major targets and avoid Confederate forces. These slaves were legally taken as refugees and provided with supplies and land. However, many others died of starvation or disease as they traveled with the Union army towards safety.

The March to the Sea decimated the Confederacy and was one of the few uses of a "scorched earth campaign" on American soil, breaking down the Confederate forces without once building a supply line to get help from the North. It was an incredible campaign but still one remembered with anger in many parts of the South.

Life on the Battlefield

Living as a soldier in either army was a perilous and painful experience, even before you got onto the battlefield.

Medicine was a disastrous situation in military camps. Nurses were totally insufficient to stop the tide of disease that swept through the camps. This was before the idea of handwashing had totally caught on with doctors, so if you didn't die of a battlefield injury and didn't die of shock during an anesthetic-free amputation, you'd probably die of infection afterwards. Amputations were the most common operation performed on the field, with around 60,000 amputations carried out by surgeons, nicknamed "sawbones." The medicine most commonly used for a painkiller was just plain alcohol, but if you had a well-supplied camp, you might be able to have some mercury with it.

The diet consisted of water, "hardtack" (a type of flat biscuit like a cracker), salt pork, corn, and beans. If you got fresh meat, it was probably from an animal killed in battle, like your horse or mule. You might be able to get some fresh food if you recently captured a city, but the odds were not in your favor.

The technology of war was also changing fast. Men still fought with swords in hand-to-hand combat, but there were also grenades and mines that could kill hundreds in a single blast. The variety of fighting tactics added a whole new level of stress to the fighting. You never knew when you could be in the middle of having a sword fight with your enemy and a grenade might go off behind you and end that fight prematurely and unchivalrously.

RANDOM FACTS

1. Taking into account all soldiers in the Civil War, the chance of a soldier surviving was about one in four.

2. Disease was an even bigger killer than fighting. About 121,000 soldiers were killed on the actual battlefields, with around 83,700 dying as a direct result of wounds soon afterwards. However, over 360,000 soldiers died of dysentery, typhoid, and pneumonia plagues that swept through the camps—95,000 of dysentery alone. And those weren't even the only diseases making their rounds in encampments, just the top three.

3. The Battle of Chickamauga had the highest number of casualties in the Western theatre and the second-highest in the whole war after Gettysburg.

4. According to some questionable but popular historical sources, the word "Chickamauga" (the name of the creek from which the Chickamauga Campaign and Battle of Chickamauga get their names) might be Cherokee for "river of death." Alternative origins have been proposed. The meaning might also be "be good," "stagnant water," or "fish-spearing place."

5. The Union army adopted the Spencer repeating rifle, which was a much faster and efficient way of killing people than a traditional rifle. They were a popular weapon during the Battle of Chickamauga and in part responsible for the high body count.

6. The Confederates did not officially adopt the Spencer repeating rifle but did capture some and use them in battle. However, by the time some fell into their hands, they were so short on supplies that they were not able to manufacture ammunition for them.

7. When it happened, the Battle of Shiloh had the highest death toll of any battle in American history, but it was soon superseded by the Battle of Antietam and the Battle of Gettysburg.

8. After the Chattanooga Campaign, a chaplain asked Union General George Henry Thomas whether he wanted the dead to be separated by state when they were buried. "Mix 'em up," Thomas told him. "I'm tired of states' rights."

9. Confederate guerrilla forces were called bushwhackers. Union guerrilla forces were called Jayhawkers.

10. Abraham Lincoln was not one of the main speakers at the Gettysburg dedication ceremony. He had the shortest speech of anyone there. His

speech is the only one history has remembered.

11. There are five known manuscripts of the Gettysburg Address in Lincoln's hand, and it's impossible to know which one ended up being read at the dedication ceremony. However, one copy was signed and dated by Lincoln, and that one usually provides the standard text (like the inscription on the Lincoln Memorial).

12. The song "Marching through Georgia" was composed by Henry Clay Work in 1865, from the point of view of a Union soldier in Sherman's March. Sherman hated the song. He thought it was tactless to be so gleeful about a scorched earth campaign, and he got annoyed that it was played at every public function he attended for the rest of his life.

13. The famous American poet Walt Whitman served as a nurse during the war.

14. Uniforms were hard to come by in the early days of the war. Hundreds of soldiers were killed by men on their own side because they were not wearing the correct color (dark blue for the Union, grey for the Confederacy).

15. Stonewall Jackson was one of those men. After all his "stone wall" behavior on the battlefield, he was shot and killed accidentally by one of his own soldiers.

16. Both sides of the Civil War developed large-scale prison camps. The Confederate camp at Andersonville imprisoned more than 30,000 soldiers, out of which around 13,000 died. The commander, Henry Wirz, was later executed for war crimes.

17. The only other person executed for war crimes in the Civil War was the Confederate guerrilla fighter Champ Ferguson.

18. A man in the Union could avoid being drafted into the army by paying $300— equivalent to around $4,000 today—to "buy" a replacement.

19. When a Union army doctor called William Hammond tried to tell his fellow doctors that the mercury they were using as medicine was poisonous, he was laughed out of his position. Literally. He was dismissed from his post for being a quack.

20. Women were, of course, not allowed in either the Union or Confederate army. However, it is estimated that up to 400 women fought in the armies while disguised as men.

Test Yourself – Questions and Answers

1. What was Sherman's March?

   a. William Tecumseh Sherman's campaign to capture Savannah, starting from Atlanta and using "scorched earth" tactics to destroy infrastructure along the way.
   b. March 1865, when William Tecumseh Sherman secured sixteen victories for the Union army.
   c. A marching formation perfected by William Tecumseh Sherman that made small armies seem much larger from a distance.

2. Which state is Chattanooga in?

   a. Georgia
   b. Tennessee
   c. South Carolina

3. What were Confederate guerrilla forces called?

   a. Backwalkers
   b. Jayhawkers
   c. Bushwhackers

4. Which disease had the highest death toll in military camps?

   a. Dysentery
   b. Typhus
   c. Pneumonia

5. Which battle had the highest death toll?

    a. The Battle of Chickamauga

    b. The Battle of Gettysburg

    c. The Battle of Antietam

Answers

1. a
2. b
3. c
4. a
5. b

CHAPTER FOUR

THE END OF THE WAR

The Emancipation Proclamation

With all the fighting, the back-and-forth between significant cities, the huge number of named battles, and the war crimes committed by both the Union and the Confederate armies, it gets easy by this point in the story to forget what the whole war had actually been about. As a reminder: slavery.

Remember, as the Civil War started, Abraham Lincoln was not one hundred percent against slavery, and he had some pretty nasty views of black people. But by 1863, he decided it was time for him to put his foot down. They were already two years into the war, so the Union might as well go all-in!

On January 1, 1863, Lincoln issued an executive order called the Emancipation Proclamation, stating that the legal status recognized by the United States of America of all enslaved people in the South become *free*. As soon as a former slave escaped the power of the Confederate government, either by crossing into Union territory or by meeting and going under the protection of a Union army, they were free, and the United States would protect their rights against any Confederates who tried to take them back.

Since the Emancipation Proclamation was being issued as a "war measure" (i.e. something with the official purpose of improving the Union's chances in war), it didn't apply to any slaves living in non-Confederate territories, but by that time, most non-Confederate territories had already recognized that the door was closing on slavery, and they were getting rid of slave laws anyway. But the Emancipation Proclamation paved the way for the next step in outlawing slavery altogether.

The Thirteenth Amendment

Almost two years after the Emancipation Proclamation, as the Union got more and more confident about a victory, it became time to lay down some laws about slavery that weren't trapped under the umbrella of "war measures." Lincoln was not going to let slave owners in the South try to get their so-called property back once the war was over, and the thirteenth amendment made one hundred percent clear exactly what kind of policy the United States were going to have on slavery once they got united again.

The Thirteenth Amendment was added on to the United States Constitution and consisted of two parts:

> One: Neither slavery nor involuntary servitude, except as a punishment for crime whereof the party shall have been duly convicted, shall exist within the United States, or any place subject to their jurisdiction.

> Two: Congress shall have power to enforce this article by appropriate legislation.

And just like that, the United States had made their statement on slavery, and the South—crumbling under the weight of military campaigns and increasingly aware that there was no way that the war was going to end in their favor—was going to have to learn to live with it.

On the Way Out

Starting with the Battle of Gettysburg, the Confederate army was suffering more and more defeats, and the defeats were turning out to have greater and greater impacts. They were losing men left and right, and their supply lines had been long since cut off. The people of the South were starving, cities were ravaged by Sherman's march and other campaigns, and the numbers of the Confederate army were so depleted that they had to start letting black people in.

Robert E. Lee had pretty much taken control of the Confederate forces, and they were stretched thin. Ulysses S. Grant had been catching him in skirmish after skirmish, not huge individual battles but ones that were frequent enough and required enough movement that Lee couldn't get his army back on its feet after one to prepare for the next.

The Surrender at Appomattox

On April 9, 1865, Robert E. Lee made one last big effort at turning the war around in the Confederates' favor. The Confederates in the Eastern Theatre had been pushed out of their makeshift capital at Richmond, Virginia, and were desperate to connect with those in the Western Theatre to regroup and make another stab at a comeback.

Lee was planning on capturing a village called Appomattox in Virginia, which he was going to use as a safe retreat. He thought that the only people from the Union there would be some foot soldiers with not-very-impressive weapons. But he was wrong. Appomattox just happened to be protected by about a hundred and fifty thousand Union soldiers against whom the Confederate forces (less than thirty thousand) didn't stand a chance.

When Lee realized the kind of forces he was standing

up against, he realized that his only option was to surrender or lose the lives of his entire army, and his own life too.

In a famous formal ceremony held in the parlor of a local grocer, Robert E. Lee signed the surrender of his Army of Northern Virginia to Ulysses S. Grant and the Union.

The Assassination

Things were looking up for the Union. With Robert E. Lee surrendered, their most skilled military enemy was out of the picture. Lincoln was confident that Lee's precedent would encourage other Confederate leaders to surrender soon too. That Good Friday, he celebrated with a trip to the theatre.

Lincoln's fateful theatre visit has been turned into an American myth. According to various stories, he was warned not to attend by his bodyguard, he didn't really want to go, his wife complained of a headache, or, alternatively, insisted that he accompany her. The play was a comedy called *Our American Cousin*, about an uncouth but honest American visiting aristocratic relatives in England. As the audience was doubled over laughing at one of the jokes, a gunshot went off in the presidential booth.

An actor and Confederate sympathizer named John Wilkes Booth jumped down onto the stage. For a moment, people thought he was part of the play, but the blood covering him was real. He shouted something—accounts vary as to what. It might have been *sic semper tyrannis*—"thus always to tyrants," the motto of the state of Virginia. It might have been "the South is avenged" or "the South shall be free." Two witnesses reported simply that he shouted, "I have done it."

Lincoln had been shot through the head. He was dead by the next day.

The Disbanding of Mosby's Raiders

Mosby's Raiders were a troupe of Confederate guerrillas who had spent the last two years trying to prevent the Union from getting a good grip on their home territory of Loudoun Valley in northwest Virginia. Their techniques included disrupting lines of supply and communication between Union armies on the field and the Federal powers in cities, and they were especially skilled at disguising themselves as regular civilians and avoiding capture.

Their leader, John S. Mosby, refused to surrender the guerrillas in any sort of traditional fashion. But on April 21st—twelve whole days after Robert E. Lee officially surrendered the Army of Northern Virginia—Mosby sent this embittered letter to the Raiders:

Soldiers!

I have summoned you together for the last time. The vision we have cherished of a free and independent country has vanished, and that country is now the spoil of a conqueror. I disband your organization in preference to surrendering it to our enemies. I am no longer your commander. After association of more than two eventful years, I part from you with a just pride, in the fame of your achievements, and grateful recollections of your generous kindness to myself. And now at this moment of bidding you a final adieu accept the assurance of my unchanging confidence and regard.

Farewell.

John S. Mosby, Col

Johnson's Proclamation

On May 9, 1865, the New York Times reported that President Andrew Johnson (who had taken over from Lincoln after the assassination) had declared that "armed resistance to the authority of the government in certain States heretofore declared to be in insurrection, may be declared as virtually at an end." Johnson's statement sent a clear message to the South: they were no longer going to be treated like a warring faction. Now, they were just criminals and terrorists. Johnson said that the government's MO was now going to be to arrest anyone found plotting with the Confederacy and to refuse entry to US ports any ships that were harboring Confederate soldiers or supplies. Anyone who tried to do *anything* under the Confederate leaders was now considered a rebel and was going to be dealt with as someone guilty of treason.

> All persons who shall exercise, claim, pretend or attempt to exercise any political, military or civil power, authority, jurisdiction or right, by, through or under JEFFERSON DAVIS, late of the City of Richmond, and his confidants, or under JOHN LETCHER or WILLIAM SMITH, and their confidants, or under any pretended political, military or civil commission or authority issued by them or of them, since the 17th day of April, 1861, shall be deemed and taken as in rebellion against the United States, and shall be dealt with accordingly.

President Davis

With the armies dropping like flies and Andrew Johnson committed to a new, harsher crackdown on Confederates, there weren't many options left for Confederacy president Jefferson Davis. He knew better than to expect he could hold out for very long against the Union without his high-powered generals like Robert E. Lee to help him. On May 5, 1865, Davis had held the last official meeting of the Confederate cabinet and declared it officially dissolved, which he had hoped—wrongly, as it turned out—would be enough to satisfy the Union.

But Johnson wasn't one to just let an enemy leader go free. He sent out his best men to track down and capture Davis so he could bring him to trial for treason. After scouting across Georgia, Union Lieutenant Colonel Benjamin D. Pritchard discovered a camp they were pretty sure belonged to Davis and charged at dawn. Davis and the soldiers at the camps were caught so off-guard that they didn't even put up a fight, and Davis immediately surrendered to the Union.

After Davis surrendered, it was just a matter of knocking out the last few pockets of resistance. Individual militias and guerrilla groups were still scattered across the South, but with no central authority, they became easier and easier to pick out. One by one, state armies and independent militias alike signed official surrenders.

Stand Watie

Stand Watie was a leader of the Cherokee Indigenous people and the last holdout for the Confederate army. That's right, there were Native American people who sided with the Confederate army as well. Watie had been leading a cavalry of Indigenous people from the Cherokee, Muskogee, and Seminole Nations, and had advanced to the rank of general within the Confederate States Army for his work leading them. He was the only Indigenous person on either side of the war to rise to such a high rank.

Most Indigenous people weren't that interested in the South's slave-holding principles, but the Cherokee people were *very* worried about the Union's interest in creating a new state out of their territory. By supporting the Confederacy, Watie and his compatriots hoped to show the Union that they were willing to stand up for their own "states' rights" and not allow their land to be taken without a fight.

As the war went on, many Cherokee people lost their interest in supporting the Confederacy, but Watie never wavered. He led a guerrilla force that became known for its strength and its brutality. Their force captured huge quantities of Union supplies and were known to massacre black people in camps.

On June 23, after years of being hunted, Watie finally surrendered—the very last Confederate general to do so.

Peace, Order, and Tranquility

On August 20, 1866, more than a year after Robert E. Lee surrendered, President Andrew Johnson signed a proclamation declaring the official end of all war hostilities. It was called *Proclamation – Declaring that*

Peace, Order, Tranquility, and Civil Authority now Exists in and Throughout the Whole of the United States of America. The Proclamation declared that the final evidence of rebellion had been stamped out in Texas, which was a state that had been full of petty skirmishes and general lawlessness since before the war. The Civil War had practically just been an excuse for crime there for some time.

With the bold declaration of "peace, order, tranquility, and civil authority," Johnson was saying that the hostilities of the war were over... but that would have been far too simple. If anything, things that had been bad for everyday people *during* the war were about to get a whole lot worse now that it was over.

Lincoln's Plan for Reconstruction

By the time the war was over—and by the time Jackson had made his declaration of "peace, order, tranquility, and civil authority"—Lincoln was long dead. But he had been working on a plan for what to do after the war, and his ideas loomed over Jackson as he developed his plan for bringing the reluctant Confederate states back into the Union.

First, Lincoln had taken a big stand on how freed ex-slaves ought to be treated by the United States. He had pushed through the Thirteenth Amendment, guaranteeing their freedom from slavery. He passed legislation that prevented discrimination based on race, and he created the Freedmen's Bureau. The Freedmen's Bureau was meant to help refugees of the war, both white and black. The main purpose of the Bureau was to integrate ex-slaves into society and help them begin to participate in United States society and politics.

But Lincoln was also conscious that all this slave-freeing and enfranchisement business was going to make former slave owners very unhappy, and so he was taking steps to make things seem not so bad for them too. After all, the former slave owners had power in the South—political power and social power. They had been able to orchestrate a rebellion once, and it could happen again. So, he planned to develop policies that would reimburse slave owners for their "lost property" (both slaves and actual property that had been destroyed in the war) and heavily offer pardons for those who had been involved in the rebellions.

Johnson's Problem

So, Lincoln's been assassinated. What does Johnson do to deal with the problem of re-integrating the Southern states back into the Union? He could just follow Lincoln's plan to the letter. Lincoln had, after all, already done the hard work of getting Congress on board with it. But Johnson wasn't Lincoln. He had his own values, his own concerns, and his own feelings about how the Southern rebels should be handed.

To summarize, Johnson was *furious* at the Confederates. He had been a leading voice in talk of hanging rebels and making them pay for the losses of the war. He had a long-standing gripe with the land-owning "plantation aristocracy" of the South, which might have something to do with the fact that he had been born into poverty in the South in 1808. His childhood memories of living in squalor while plantation owners lounged around forcing slaves do all their work *might* have had something to do with his plans for what was going to happen after the war.

But Johnson also had to be practical. The South was packed with angry, embittered ex-rebels, and hanging all of them would have left the country in shambles. No, the South had to be reintegrated back into the Union as quickly as possible, with as little violence as possible.

The Fourteenth Amendment: Rights for Americans of All Colours

As hundreds of thousands of black Americans were legally freed from slavery, questions began to pop up about how they should be treated. Did being "not enslaved" mean that they were legally equal to white Americans? Remember, Lincoln (and plenty of other high-profile anti-slavery advocates before the war) had pretty negative views of black people. The pseudo-science of the day insisted that black people were *medically* inferior to White people. If, as the science went, a black person was *scientifically*, *objectively* less intelligent than a white person, in the same way that a child is *scientifically*, *objectively* less intelligent than an adult, then wouldn't it be the best thing to do, to prevent black people from participating in public life, politics, or all the other things that it takes lots of brains to deal with? The idea that the "science" saying black people were inferior might just be *wrong* hadn't occurred to many people.

On July 9, 1868, an amendment was created that was meant to address the rights of all American citizens — black or white. It had five different sections, but it was the first one that stated that:

All persons born or naturalized in the United States, and subject to the jurisdiction thereof, are citizens of the United States and of the State wherein they reside. No State shall make or enforce any law which shall abridge the privileges or immunities of citizens of the United States; nor shall any State deprive any person of life, liberty, or property, without due process of law; nor deny to any person within its jurisdiction the equal protection of the laws.

The further sections made laws about how Americans

would be represented in the government, and how people rebelling against the government would be treated, but it was that first one that was the most controversial. Here, at last, was a law saying *no*, you *can't* treat people of any color any differently just because of their skin. It was a huge step forward.

How well did it work? Well… not quite as well as planned.

The Fifteenth Amendment

Even though the Fourteenth Amendment said that all people born or naturalized in the United States were citizens and no law could limit their rights, it still took a whole extra amendment to make one *hundred* percent clear that former slaves were supposed to have the right to vote. In fact, this amendment probably wouldn't have even gotten made, and states would have been able to go on making state laws that prevented black men from being able to vote, except that former Union general Ulysses S. Grant became President of the United States in 1868. He realized that if he wanted to be re-elected, or if he wanted his party to have any staying power, he was going to need more loyal voters, and he was pretty sure the black community would be loyal voters. After all, their other option was the pro-slavery Democrat Party.

So, Grant and the United States Congress put together

an amendment that *finally* gave voting rights to black men, by saying:

> The rights of citizen of the United States to vote shall not be denied or abridged by the United States or by any State on account of race, color, or previous condition of servitude.

This was the third of three amendments known as the "Reconstruction Amendments," laws put in place to limit racism in the South and clarify the United States' position on slavery once and for all.

Radical Republicans

We'll get into the politics of Reconstruction more in the next chapter, but for now, let's add one more player to the game. On one side, there's Andrew Johnson: bitter about the plantation aristocracy, with pretty negative views towards former slave-owners, but eager to get the South back into the Union without having to kill anyone. On the other side, there are the former Confederates: also bitter, recently defeated, panicked about whether they're all going to be hanged, and as a side note, anyone who owned slaves now suddenly doesn't and has to figure out what they're going to do about their massively oversized plantation that was only economically viable if they had basically infinite free labour.

And then a third group bangs in: a faction of the Republican Party that had been active since before the war. The self-styled Radical Republicans went a few steps beyond the likes of Johnson or Lincoln. They had absolutely no sympathy for slave owners or slavery and were eager to see the whole lifestyle abolished and civil rights for slaves brought in to replace them.

As Lincoln had gone about preparing his policy, Radical Republicans had pushed him at every turn for a more aggressive stance towards rebels, and Lincoln had blocked their every effort to create their own legislation, keeping them in a stalemate. The Radical Republicans had thought that Johnson would be on their side and prosecute the Southern leaders harshly, and were shocked and disappointed that he seemed more interested in reunification than retribution. By the time the papers had been signed and the war was over, they were chomping at the bit to get their vision of justice for the South enacted.

RANDOM FACTS

1. The grocer in whose house the surrender of Appomattox was signed was named Wilmer McLean. He hadn't always been an Appomattox resident. He used to own a plantation. But four years earlier, he had decided to abandon that plantation after his home was used by the Confederates as a headquarters during the First Battle of Bull Run. That's right, McLean's houses got borrowed by war efforts not once but *twice*, in two completely different cities and situations.

2. There was a Union General named Jefferson Davis, the same name as the Confederate President. The Union army took a hit at the Battle of Chickamauga when they heard a troop say they were "Jeff Davis's troops" and assumed that they meant the *Union* Jeff Davis.

3. Robert E. Lee might have been a stone-cold killer on the battlefield, but his cook, a slave named William Mack Lee, claimed that he was an animal lover. Apparently, Robert E. Lee had a pet hen that he had been given by a farmer in Virginia, and the only time Robert ever scolded William (according to his testimony) was when William killed the bird for a celebratory dinner.

4. The inventor of Coca-Cola, John Stith Pemberton, was wounded in one of the last battles of the Civil War. This led to his interest in drinks that could serve as painkillers, and his eventual development of Coca-Cola—in its original, cocaine-containing form.

5. John Munson, one of Mosby's Raiders, describes their technique of disguising themselves as civilians, tipping off neither Union nor Confederate forces: "'Something gray' was the one requisite of our dress, and the cost of it mattered little... It has been said that we wore blue to deceive the enemy, but this is ridiculous, for we were always in the enemy's country where a Southern soldier caught dressed in a blue uniform would have been treated to a swift court-martial and shot as a spy... We had no reason to use a blue uniform as a disguise, for there was no occasion to do so. Many of our attacks were made at night, when all colors looked alike, and in daytime we did not have to deceive the Yankees in order to get at them."

6. John Wilkes Booth had planned to execute Ulysses S. Grant at the same time as he executed Lincoln. He had heard that they were going to be at the theatre together, but there was a last-minute change of plans and Grant didn't end up being there. The reason? Grant's wife Julia and

Lincoln's wife Mary didn't get along and didn't want to have to sit next to each other during the play. Remember, pettiness saves lives!

7. John Wilkes Booth's plot assassination of Lincoln was only one-third of a plan to kill the major Union political figures. The Secretary of State William Seward and the Vice President Andrew Johnson were both supposed to die too. Booth was the only one who managed to actually hit his target. Seward was injured but recovered, and the man who was supposed to assassinate Johnson lost his nerve.

8. Mary Surratt, one of the people involved in planning Lincoln's assassination, was the first woman to be hanged by the US government.

9. When Jefferson Davis was captured, his wife devised a plan to try to get him out. She asked the guard who was watching their tent if she and her mother could go fetch some water, which the guard allowed. The two women left and were heading down for the river when the guard noticed that the mother was wearing men's boots. They were almost out of the camp before the guard caught up, demanded that the mother pull back her scarf, and revealed Davis dressed in women's clothing.

10. Tallahassee, Florida, was the only Confederate

state capital east of the Mississippi that wasn't captured by Union forces.

11. Andrew Johnson had served as an indentured servant as a child. He and his brother ran away from their owner after two years.

12. Andrew Johnson was the first-ever US president to be impeached, meaning he was legally charged with "high crimes and misdemeanors," but the Senate chose not to convict him, meaning that the impeachment didn't mean he actually had to leave office. He left office normally.

13. Johnson's impeachment was out-voted by only one vote.

14. When the Fifteenth Amendment was being drafted, there were plans to make it even more comprehensive, maybe even giving voting rights to women and to Indigenous people (neither of whom were allowed to vote yet).

15. Only twenty-eight of the states needed to ratify (agree to) an amendment in order for it to be passed. Twenty-nine ratified the Fifteenth Amendment. The other seven rejected it at the time but ratified it later.

16. Tennessee was the last of the thirty-eight states to ratify the fifteenth amendment... in *1997*. That's right: almost *a hundred and thirty years* after it was proposed.

17. The first known black man to cast a vote after the Fifteenth Amendment was ratified was named Thomas Mundy Peterson. He lived in New Jersey.

18. United States Supreme Court was pretty stingy closing loopholes that prevented black people from voting. In the case "*United States v. Reese*" in 1876, the Supreme Court claimed that the Fifteenth Amendment didn't *give* black people the right to vote, it just meant that being black (or an ex-slave) couldn't be the (only) reason they *weren't* allowed to vote. They still had to meet other voting requirements, no matter how unfair those requirements were.

19. It wasn't until the 1910s that the Supreme Court started having a broader interpretation of the Fifteenth Amendment and started looking more critically at voting requirements that targeted Black voters.

20. Forty percent of the men killed in the Civil War were never identified.

Test Yourself – Questions and Answers

1. When did Robert E. Lee surrender?

    a. April 1, 1864
    b. April 9, 1865
    c. April 20, 1866

2. Which of these Confederate leaders was the first to officially surrender?

    a. John S. Mosby
    b. Stand Watie
    c. Robert E. Lee

3. What play was Abraham Lincoln watching when he was assassinated?

    a. *Hamlet* by William Shakespeare
    b. *Our American Cousin* by Tom Taylor
    c. *The Importance of Being Earnest* by Oscar Wilde

4. Who were the Radical Republicans?

    a. Republicans who supported civil rights for former slaves and harsh prosecution for former slave owners
    b. Republicans who supported the Confederacy's right to secede
    c. Republicans who were very cool

5. Which state was the last to ratify the Fifteenth Amendment?

   a. Tennessee
   b. Georgia
   c. Mississippi

Answers

1. b
2. c
3. b
4. a
5. a

CHAPTER FIVE

THE PROBLEM OF RECONSTRUCTION

The war was won, but the conflict was far from over. In fact, for many people living in the South, it seemed like the worst was yet to come. The federal (Union) government was making a plan for how to "fix" or "reconstruct" the South after the Civil War, and even on paper, it didn't look good for the former planter aristocracy. And in practice, it ended up being even worse for them.

What was Reconstruction?

On top of that, the South had just lost the mainstay of its economy. Without slaves, the agrarian system that had been the center of the entire economy just wasn't going to work. Massive plantations couldn't pay for actual wages for the workers. It just wasn't going to happen. Now, the South was filled with thousands of freshly freed slaves, a good chunk of extremely disgruntled former owners, and plenty of people who were still not one hundred percent okay with the idea of being part of the Union at all.

So, what was the Union going to do to deal with that tension? They couldn't just send the Southern states back to normal. The people who had held political power were the former slave owners, and if they were allowed to have power again, they had every reason to just rebel again or try to create new legislation that would get their slaves back or otherwise cause trouble.

But it also wouldn't be practical for the Union to just put the former Confederacy under a perpetual state of martial law. That would be expensive, difficult to manage, and probably lead to all sorts of new tensions, and, again, an upcoming rebellion.

So, the leaders of the United States devised a plan. They would develop a process for getting the South back on its feet. They would take power away from people who would cause trouble and in their place create a new solid economy and government that would prevent the Southern states from totally collapsing. They would integrate former slaves and former slave owners into a healthy society modeled by the North.

If you've heard anything about Reconstruction, you'll already know that this didn't work out as planned.

Fair Play

For us—and for the Union leaders who were charged with creating a plan for Reconstruction—it seemed fair that the South should get a pretty rough time. After all, the war was their fault. They were the ones who started it by seceding, and they were the ones who had been so committed to slavery (which we can all agree is a human rights violation, no matter how important it is to your economy). So, it wasn't that hard for people in the North to get on board with the idea of treating the South fairly harshly during Reconstruction.

Lincoln, back in his day, had been very conscious of the way that a difficult Reconstruction would breed resentment in the South, and when he developed his plan, he tried to take that into account. But he turned out to be in the minority. Not only did Johnson have a vendetta against plantation aristocracy, and not only were the Radical Republicans dedicated to an anti-slave society, but the popular opinion in the North was simply not very favorable towards the former Confederacy. No matter what one's opinions were on issues like civil rights, or even the basic idea of reunification, everyone in the North was pretty embittered towards the people who had killed their husbands, brothers, and friends in battle.

It's hard not to take the Union's side. It's hard to see

things from the perspective of people who fought and died for slavery while still remembering how morally wrong they were. But during this chapter, we're going to have to see things from the perspective not just of the Confederate politicians and soldiers, not just of the people who fought for a separate slave society, but of the common people who lived in the South—who maybe supported the Confederacy or maybe didn't—who were now facing the reality that the North was making decisions (and not generally very favourable decisions) about how they were going to be treated.

The Reconciliationist Vision

Most people on both sides of the war were, ultimately, glad for the whole thing to be over. They might want to see justice done against leaders of the Confederacy, they might want to help develop a new economy for the South, or they might want to forget the whole thing happened, but the one thing they definitely didn't want was more violence or a repeat of the war.

In the South, this led to the development of the idea of the "New South," a South with modern ideas and cultural values, integrated with the North and separate from the agrarian "Old South" that had been the basis of the Confederacy. The New South would have a diverse economy like the North. It would be the home of major urban centers. Industrialization, political scientists and commenters of the day argued, would bring prosperity to the South by giving former slaves productive work to do. By developing an industrialized economy—where a "planter aristocracy" wouldn't rule—they believed they could create a future full of racial and class harmony... or at least no *less* racial or class harmony than the North enjoyed.

Some reconciliationists were a lot less optimistic than that Radical Republicans seeking justice could fall under this umbrella too. In their opinions, the damage from the war could be healed when those responsible for it (the wealthy slave owners and politicians of the Confederacy) were duly punished and a new, less corrupt government put in place.

The Emancipationist Vision

There was another vision of Reconstruction, focussed mostly among politically active Northerners, Radical Republicans, and the occasional abolitionist Southerner. That view was focussed on emancipation as the main goal of Reconstruction. They wanted to deal with the fact that a huge segment of society (more than half the population in some regions) had just been given control over their own lives for the first time ever. People whose every action, from when they woke up in the morning to whether they were allowed to get married, had previously been dictated by others now had access to a whole host of new rights. It was a sweeping, oftentimes challenging, change.

While reconciliationists tended to focus on the politics and economics of Reconstruction, emancipationists were more interested in the social effects of the Civil War, specifically, the social effects on previously enslaved black people in the South.

These were the people pushing forward on ideas like the Fifteenth Amendment (which, remember, didn't come about until well into Reconstruction) and trying to make real positive change for the black Southern community. And, maybe unsurprisingly, they were probably the most controversial.

The White Supremacist Vision

The reaction to emancipation in the South was not pretty. Remember, unlike slavery in many civilizations, in the American South, slavery was justified by a very strong pseudo-scientific belief in certain rules of racial superiority. People in the South weren't just angry about emancipation because they felt like their property was being taken away. They were also angry that people who they considered their absolute inferiors were getting help from the government.

This led to the development of groups in the South

that were explicitly dedicated to furthering a vision of the South where white people were the undisputed dominant group. They made distinct efforts, not only to put forward political changes that would keep white people on top, but also to strike fear into the hearts of black Southerners. This was when terrorist groups like the Ku Klux Klan came into prominence and when the South gained its still-active reputation for violence against black citizens.

People with the white supremacist vision of Reconstruction were bitter about the loss for symbolic, rather than just economic or practical, reasons, and because of that their voices rang louder and had endured for longer than many reconciliationists. The feeling—sometimes explicit, sometimes unspoken—that white Southerners were somehow being *persecuted* by laws protecting black Southerners has persisted into the twentieth and even the twenty-first centuries.

The Union Government in the South

As Confederate states surrendered and came back under the power of the Union government, Lincoln (and later Johnson) experimented with different types of government in the ex-Confederacy. In South Carolina, Lincoln distributed ceded land to former slaves, but the majority of Southern states were put under the rulership of provisional Union governments.

These governments were responsible for instituting a "republican form of government," a government that would address the needs of the people and make sure power was not going back into the hands of the planter aristocracy. Johnson and the North as a whole were extremely conscious of the role of economics in developing the Confederacy, and they made moves to take power away from traditional holders and put it into the hands of industrial economic leaders, as judged by the North to be "good Republicans." Later scholars have argued that this was a power play on the part of the Northern industrialists, since industrialists were able to pass money-making measures against the South.

In 1867, the provisional governments that Lincoln had set up were replaced by martial law enforced by the Union army. They determined who could vote and who could run for office—i.e. ex-slaves could vote and ex-leaders of the Confederacy *couldn't* run for office.

Presidential Reconstruction

We've already taken a look at Johnson's vision of Reconstruction with the main goal of getting the former Confederacy back into the Union as quickly as possible. This didn't actually take him very long. In fact, by the fall of 1865, just months after the fighting had ended and people signed their surrenders,

Johnson declared that Reconstruction was completed because the country was reunified and slavery was over. That was the only goal, right?

Congress disagreed with Johnson's evaluation of "Presidential Reconstruction," a Reconstruction plan created by Johnson himself, as president. They had a whole different interpretation of how things needed to go in the South in order to get it fully reintegrated into the North's political and economic world. They called their vision "Congressional Reconstruction."

In 1866, the Radical Republicans took control of Congress. Republicans formed a majority, and Radical Republicans were common enough in that majority that they were able to get past any vetoes that Johnson tried to pull on them. In other words, short of Johnson cracking down and making himself look like a total dictator by exercising his presidential power against basically everything Congress did, Congress could re-do Reconstruction the way they wanted to.

Radical Reconstruction

Congressional Reconstruction, also known as "Radical Reconstruction," became the order of the day in 1867. Remember, "radical" was not an insult. It was what the anti-slavery Republicans actually identified themselves as. These were the people who wanted big changes in the South, the ones who put the United

States army into place, and the ones who pushed through new voting laws and restrictions. Their vision of Reconstruction had a much more active federal government and was going to mean that states could get away with a lot less when it came to trying to reconstitute their old, pre-war way of life.

Some of the goals that Radical Reconstruction focussed on included creating a "biracial state" with sufficient facilities to accommodate both black and white populations and their respective needs. They also developed a series of programs to try to improve general quality of life in the South, both for the former slaves and for the huge impoverished white community. For example, the Union government-funded public schools in the South and repaired (and generally improved) the transportation infrastructure that was damaged during the war, like the train lines. In order to fund this, they raised taxes, working towards a more socially equitable South.

Carpetbaggers and Scalawags

The army wasn't just enforcing these changes on unwilling Southerners. The South was filled with people (both originally from the North and native to the South) who supported Reconstruction. People from the North were referred to (by anti-Reconstruction Southerners) as "carpetbaggers," implying that they were coming into the South with all their belongings in a carpetbag, trying to make changes without really understanding what they were doing. Even more scathingly, pro-Reconstruction Southerners were known as "scalawags" and were often looked very harshly upon for what was perceived as a betrayal of Southern values like white supremacy. And calling white supremacy a "Southern value" isn't a modern editorial. That was actually what Democrats in the South called it.

If these names sound vaguely insulting to you, that's because they were meant to be insults. However, modern historians have generally adopted the terms to refer to supporters of Reconstruction, no matter the historians' personal positive or negative view on Reconstruction as a political policy. They're generally used neutrally today. However, in his wildly popular history book *Lies my Teacher Told Me*, James W. Loewen argues (inspired by historians like Eric Foner) that it's irresponsible to use these words without acknowledging that they were originally meant as insults. Without understanding that, it would be easy to appear like you're taking the anti-Reconstructionist' side, whether or not you actually believe in that. If you need any more proof that the names assigned to political groups at this time were heavily skewed towards Democratic sympathies, maybe you should know that Democrats who *opposed* Reconstruction were (and still are) called "Redeemers."

Black People in Politics

Over the last hundred years, historians have called into question how much political power black people were actually given in the Reconstruction South, and the consensus is not that much. But more than they had before.

In the late nineteenth and early twentieth centuries, historians tended to view the fact that black people were suddenly given the right to vote as one of the reasons for the political turmoil in the South during the Reconstruction period and after. They argued that there were problems with introducing a new voter base that hadn't been educated and didn't have much experience with politics. For example, they argued, corrupt politicians could make claims to black voters that they had no way of following through on, and the voters, being unfamiliar with the system, might not be aware that those promises were faulty. These new voters might also simply not take into account all the factors they had to deal with when making a political decision, and thus make short-sighted decisions that made sense at the time but would have negative consequences in the long term.

These historians (mostly) weren't *trying* to be racist. In fact, many of them took a fairly sympathetic view towards ex-slaves who were suddenly handed the powerful tool of the vote. But from a modern perspective, that move kind of just looks like you're foisting the blame on black people.

Remember the controversy about the Fifteenth Amendment? Black people weren't necessarily *given* the vote—being black was just no longer an acceptable reason to *deny* them the vote—so the black voting base was still a minority compared to white people in the South. Corrupt government action, therefore, can't be blamed on any one color of people. More likely, there was corruption for the same reason there always is after a major conflict—people were confused, angry, and had conflicting visions about how to solve the problem. A new, poorly-educated voter base probably didn't make things *better*, but it certainly can't take the blame.

The Ku Klux Klan

Speaking of angry and corrupt, in 1865, a terrorist group called the Ku Klux Klan—the KKK—made its debut in the South. This group was aligned with the Democrat Party of the time (although the Democrats certainly weren't taking responsibility for the crimes that the KKK was carrying out) and its central goal was simple: reinstate white supremacy in the South. This meant getting rid of the Republican government and also getting rid of as many black people as possible.

The KKK was founded in Tennessee by six former Confederate officers. According to contemporaneous reporters, for the first couple months, the group was fairly innocuous. They were secretive and had bizarre rituals but were no more secretive or bizarre than any other fraternity or "secret society." But the 1907 *Cyclopaedia of Fraternities* wrote that, starting in 1867, the KKK's focus changed. "They had played with an engine of power and mystery," the Encyclopedia wrote, "and found themselves overcome by a belief that something must lie behind it all—that there was, after all, a serious purpose, a work for the Klan to do."

The KKK spread across the South with little central authority, but groups claiming the name popping up under all states that were part of Reconstruction. They acted as vigilantes, threatening, murdering, and destroying the property of free black people, their allies, and anyone who supported or looked kindly on the Reconstruction agenda.

Sharecropping

With the freeing of slaves in the South, massive plantations were without labor, but the products they had once produced were still in demand. As the South struggled to get back on its feet, many people (on all parts of the political spectrum) agreed that it was a good idea to try to reopen those plantations for business. But, as we've clearly established, the whole reason that slavery was popular in the first place was that it wasn't economically viable to actually pay people living wages to work on a huge plantation.

So, plantation owners met with a dilemma. They legally couldn't just *own* people to work on their farms anymore, but they also couldn't afford to pay people actual *wages* to work either. What to do?

Thus, the idea of sharecropping became popular. This technique goes back to the ancient world, and to the former plantation owners, it seemed to be the answer to all their woes.

Sharecropping simply means that an owner of a large piece of land allows multiple people to live on their land for free. Those multiple people farm the land, produce crops, and sell them, and then give a portion of the profits back to the people who own the land.

So, the people in charge of plantation land divided it up and "allowed" former slaves and impoverished white families to live on it. At the onset, getting land to live on without having to put money down seemed great for these penniless families, but it quickly became clear that the sharecropping system was easy to exploit. The owners of the land could demand as large a percentage of the profit as they wanted, keeping the people actually doing the work in constant poverty. Besides that, the owners could evict their tenants at any moment for any reason (or no reason at all), keeping them in a perpetual state of anxiety and forcing them to bow and scrape to try to avoid "angering" the landowners so that they could keep their homes.

The Panic of 1873

Towards the tail end of Reconstruction, a serious economic depression hit the South. This seemed to fly in the face of every assurance that Reconstruction would save the South from the inevitable economic ruin of being an agrarian, single-crop area. The price of cotton tanked, and the industrial structures that had been put in place by the Reconstruction government were powerless to change that.

The landowners who had been creating sharecropping empires now had even more reason to try to spread the responsibility around, since owning land became a risky venture, and people who had formerly been advocating on behalf of the tenant farmers who were forced to work the land now hardly had a leg to stand on.

Besides that, with almost ten years since the abolition of slavery, abolitionist and pro-black voices were fading away. Many felt like they weren't needed anymore or that their goals had been achieved, and that was that. Republicans in the South slowly migrated North or started to shift towards a less focused political platform.

For their part, black Southerners were dealing with their newfound political autonomy in the way any group would—by internally dividing as individuals developed their own senses of political morality. Without a strong centralized voice from the black community, and with more and more restrictions being placed on their voting rights, it became even harder to enact change in their favor. The optimism of Reconstruction was quickly sputtering to a close.

The Compromise of 1877

In 1876, there was another presidential election—one of the most controversial in American history. The Democrat candidate, Samuel J. Tilden, won the popular vote, but as we all know from a recent election, the popular vote doesn't get presidents elected in America. When it came to the electoral college vote, Tilden won 184 votes, and the Republican, Rutherford B. Hayes, won 165, but twenty votes were unresolved, meaning that, technically, Hayes *might* have beaten Tilden. It was impossible to know.

So, how were people going to decide who became president? They *could* carry out the entire election again, but that would take months, and it might result in exactly the same problem. To avoid that issue, the two parties struck a deal. Hayes could be president, but he was going to have to do some things for Tilden and the Democrats first.

If Hayes wanted to be president, the Democrats said, all the federal troops that had been put in place in the South for Reconstruction needed to leave. Power had to go back into the hands of the Democrats who were running in the South. And if those Democrats then wanted to do things like, say, pass laws that disenfranchised black voters or support a sharecropping economy, then the Republicans were just going to have to deal with it.

And so they did.

Redemption

After hearing about the violence and controversy of Reconstruction, if you learned that the period following Reconstruction was called "Redemption," you might think that it was a period in which white supremacy died out, violence receded, and a balanced, biracial society was achieved. And you would be very, very wrong.

The period after Reconstruction was called "Redemption" not by optimistic contemporary historians but by Democratic Southerners who were finally able to scramble back into power after the end of Republican control and the end of Northern military presence in the South. During the 1880s and 1890s, white (and white supremacist) politicians regained practically all the power in the South and set about creating a whole new set of laws that would benefit them. They put new restrictions on black voters, ones that created loopholes around the law that forbade excluding someone from voting for being black. They also pushed forward with segregation and structured society to force black people into second-class living conditions and prevent them from interacting with white people. And anytime anyone tried to say to these politicians, "Hey, do you think it's necessary to treat black people so badly?" all they had to do was point to Reconstruction and say, "Look! Look how terrible things were then! *That's* what happens when we let black people have political power. Do you want to go back to that?"

And, for the most part, it worked. The United States might not have backtracked all the way to plantations and slavery, but black people who were alive during "Redemption" faced a whole new series of equally serious problems.

RANDOM FACTS

1. In 1870, the federal government passed laws called the Enforcement Acts, specifically targeting the Ku Klux Klan, that intended to make it possible to more effectively prosecute them for their crimes.

2. The Ku Klux Klan is still active today, taking strong inspiration from the Nazis and broadening their targets to include Jewish people, Muslims, recent immigrants, and Catholics, as well as black people and left-leaning political leaders.

3. There were multiple other white supremacist terrorist groups in the South, like the White League and the Red Shirts, but none of them had the staying power of the KKK. The KKK is the only one that remains active and prominent today.

4. The White League, also known as the White Man's League, was made up of Confederate veterans.

5. Reconstruction was a fertile time for politically-themed, introspective writing from both South and North. The prolific Kentucky poet Madison

Cawein was known for his romantic tales of King Arthur, but many of his *thousands* of poems were either directly or metaphorically about the fall of the "Old South."

6. The 1876 election of Rutherford B. Hayes had the highest voter turnout of any American election — 81.8%

7. It was also one of only five elections in which the winner of the popular vote did not win the election; 2016 was also one.

8. It was a surprise to many people that Hayes was elected president, since he was not a well-known person outside of Ohio, his home state. The contemporaneous writer and historian Henry Adams wrote that Hayes's "only recommendations are that he is obnoxious to no one."

9. It had been a crime for slaves to learn how to read and write during the South, but of the black men who became involved in politics or held office during Reconstruction, around 80% were literate.

10. A governmental group called the Freedmen's Bureau was established to help former slaves adjust to life as free men and women, including helping them find paying work and decent education.

11. The Freedmen's Bureau never had more than a thousand agents working in it at any given time.

12. Education was highly prized in the black community during Reconstruction. In the 1869 *Eighth Semi-Annual Report on Schools for Freedmen* published by the federal government, an elderly black man excitedly reported that his former master only ever read him the parts of the Bible about obedience, and he was thrilled to now be able to read the *entire* Bible.

13. Writer and activist W. E. B. Du Bois put his finger on the anxiety of white supremacists during Reconstruction when he said, "there was only one thing that the white South feared more than negro dishonesty, ignorance, and incompetence, and that was negro honesty, knowledge, and efficiency." The restrictions put on education and self-improvement opportunities for black people during and after Reconstruction proved that.

14. Historians of the twentieth century focussed almost single-mindedly on the turmoil of Reconstruction. John W. Burgess called it "the most soul-sickening spectacle that Americans had ever been called upon to behold," and Claude G. Bowers said that "southern people were literally put to the torture" during Reconstruction.

15. Reconstruction was the first time that a "redistribution of wealth" plan was put into action by a federal government. This type of plan would become much more strongly associated with communism in the twentieth century.

16. Starting in 1865, but developing throughout Reconstruction and after, Southern states created "Black Codes" that restricted the freedoms of former slaves. These Codes included restrictions on when they could travel, whether they could own firearms, what kind of work they could do, and even how they were punished for crimes (usually more harshly than white people).

17. If a black person was convicted for a crime and unable to pay a fine, they were sent to work in chain gangs—essentially forced labor for the state government—doing work like rebuilding railways or other infrastructure.

18. The Black Codes formed the foundation for the "Jim Crow" laws of the early twentieth century, which were the United States' official segregation laws.

19. Congress was not happy about the Black Codes and blamed Johnson for being too lenient on the South and allowing them to happen. However, they could not constitutionally reverse the codes.

20. If the United States government had reimbursed

all Southern slave owners for the cost of their slaves instead of fighting the Civil War, it would have cost the government *one-tenth* of the price, not to mention all the lives.

Test Yourself – Questions and Answers

1. When did Reconstruction take place?

   a. 1860-1865
   b. 1865-1877
   c. 1877-1890

2. Which of these white supremacist terrorist organizations is still active today?

   a. The White League
   b. The Red Shirts
   c. The Ku Klux Klan

3. What was the Panic of 1873?

   a. An economic depression
   b. A riot that led to the deaths of 327 free black men and women
   c. An incident in which psychoactive fungus poisoned the water supply of Richmond, Virginia, the former Confederate capital

4. What is sharecropping?

   a. The practice of tenant farmers living on land owned by someone else and "paying" the owner with a portion of their farm profits
   b. The practice of dividing a town's total yield of crops evenly between households
   c. A popular hairstyle where hair is cropped around the ears

5. Approximately what percentage of black politically active men were literate during Reconstruction?

   a. 20%
   b. 50%
   c. 80%

Answers

1. b
2. c
3. a
4. a
5. c

CHAPTER SIX

THE LEGACY OF THE CIVIL WAR

Considering the sheer scale of the Civil War, the number of named battles, the number of people killed, the still-present racial tensions in the United States, and the unresolved conflicts of Reconstruction, is there any wonder that the Civil War is one of the most prominent wars in American thinking? Unlike some wars—like World War One and World War Two—it's hard to say that the Civil War led to a sudden sweeping change in people's behavior or another obvious political event. But it became embedded in American culture and remains a massive touchstone for anyone discussing politics, especially in the South.

The Civil War in the Press

The Civil War didn't just make a big impact on America because of its scale and hot-button issues. It also made a big impact on America because it was reported more thoroughly than any other previous war.

In the mid-1800s, literacy was becoming more important. Both the United States and England were in the process of expanding their education systems so that more people—especially lower-class people—were able to read. With more people able to read, more people were interested in keeping up with current events in the newspapers, which meant that more people were hearing more about the Civil War and the political events surrounding it.

Now, as careful as we have to be in 2018 about "fake news," "fake news" was infinitely more difficult to spot in 1860. With no internet and no way to easily contact political representatives, newspapers could basically get away with printing anything. While there were many papers dedicated to reporting fairly and accurately about the War, there were many more that printed sensationalist stories to drive up sales. Besides that, there were also loads of reputable papers that printed more or less accurate information but did it in a very biased way, focussing on the crimes of the other side or leaving out negative things about the side the paper supported.

Papers printed illustrations of events and political cartoons caricaturing leaders, but they also revolutionized war coverage by printing photographs of soldiers, battlefields, and dead bodies. Printing photos made these papers seem even more reliable. After all, a camera doesn't lie.

The photos and newspaper articles give modern historians a great insight into the War, but they also affected how average people at the time perceived it. If you lived in the North, you would definitely be reading a lot of scathing articles about the evils of the South, and if you lived in the South, Sherman's March would get a lot more press than Robert E. Lee's tactics. The press helped harden public opinions about the Civil War and has continued to affect how we see it today.

Jim Crow Laws

We saw "Jim Crow" laws mentioned above, but what exactly were they?

"Jim Crow" laws were a set of laws about segregation that came into place in the period after the Civil War, after Reconstruction, starting with "Redemption" and carrying well into the twentieth century. These laws dictated where black people could go, what they could do, and when and how they could interact with white people. They got their name from a song and dance called "Jump Jim Crow" done by a white actor named Thomas D. Rice, who wore blackface and caricatured stereotypical black mannerisms.

The laws started out patchy. A town here or a county there would pass laws saying that black people couldn't use a white school, hotel, or other facility. In 1892, a man named Homer Plessey, a light-skinned man with one black grandparent, tested the railway's rules about separating white and black (or mixed-race) passengers. He bought a first-class ticket and sat in the "whites-only car" and was arrested when he refused to move.

Plessey's case brought segregation to national attention, and the Supreme Court ruled, in 1896, that it was constitutional to require black people to use "separate but equal" facilities from white people. Everyone remembered the "separate" part, but no one was watching out to make sure the facilities really were "equal." Because of that, black Americans were subjected to decades of subpar transportation, living accommodations, and schooling, and had no one who would listen to them when they pointed out that there was nothing "equal" about the way they were being treated.

Civil War Veterans

World War One, fifty years after the end of the Civil War, was the first time that the effects of war on survivors was really studied. The term "post-traumatic stress disorder" wasn't coined until the Vietnam War. However, the Civil War paved the way for that newfound understanding of the negative effects of combat on veterans. Remember, the Civil War had a huge number of American casualties, rivaling the number of Americans killed in the World Wars. And unlike those, it was taking place "at home," so even more young people and families were affected by it. The sheer numbers, and the numbers of people who might not otherwise get involved in combat, meant that the issue of dealing with veterans after the war was on a much bigger scale than it ever had been in America before.

Earlier wars, in the broad public imagination, were generally positive events (at least, for the winners). Combat was mostly hand-to-hand, and fighting in a war was a wonderful, healthy, moral way to prove your bravery and manliness. War wasn't *exactly* seen as a good thing, but there were certainly a lot of positive ideas about it floating around.

Not so much in the Civil War. The scale of killing and the new industrial weapons made the idea of displaying bravery in hand-to-hand combat a lot less realistic. The Indiana Hospital for the Insane reported that 300 veterans were committed for nervous breakdowns or other psychological problems. A Texas man named George Gautier, who served in the Confederate army, wrote a memoir called *Harder than Death*, which might be the first book that pins down what we'd now call post-traumatic stress disorder.

While some historians have argued that the nineteenth-century view of death was much more matter-of-fact than ours, and thus that Civil War soldiers probably weren't as terrified of dying as modern people, Gautier's memoirs and the numbers of people committed to the insane asylum seem to say otherwise.

Re-enactments

Sometimes when the Civil War comes up today, it's in the context of serious issues like whether the Confederate flag should be considered a symbol that incites violence. But sometimes, the Civil War comes up in a much lighter context!

Civil War re-enactments are one of the most popular forms of historical roleplay or "living history" in the world. Obviously, it's most popular in the United States, but there are also groups in Canada, the UK, Germany, Italy, and Poland, all dedicated to re-enacting battles and events from the American Civil War.

What is a Civil War re-enactment? It's an activity where people dress up as either specific characters (like Abraham Lincoln or Robert E. Lee) or fictional civilians (like soldiers, wives, farmers, slaves, et cetera) and "act out" events of the Civil War. Often, they recreate battles, walking through tactics, sometimes repeating scripts (when specific quotes or speeches are known), or filling in the blanks with how they *think* people would have acted. Sometimes, they also portray everyday life in a camp or town during the Civil War.

Sometimes these enactments are open to the public for educational purposes, but sometimes they are closed in order to totally immerse the re-enactors in the life of the 1860s. Both types are wildly popular and attended by huge numbers of people every year.

Southern Gothic

To many people, the Civil War cemented the idea that the American South was a distinct society that was unique—maybe even irreconcilably so—from the Northern states. To many Northerners, the fact that Southerners would live and die to support slavery showed, without a doubt, that this was a corrupted society.

If there's one group of people who love the idea of a corrupted society, it's artists. In the twentieth century, a genre of literature (and film and art) called "Southern gothic" developed to explore this perceived corruption. "Gothic" literature (and film and art) was an eighteenth- and nineteenth-century genre that used horror elements to thrill readers and explore the dark side of beautiful or romantic images.

It was only natural that this genre would appeal to

people wanting to explore the South. What better beautiful or romantic image to explore the dark side of than the pre-Civil War American South? More than traditional British gothic literature, the Southern gothic genre tended to be politically themed. The corruption it displayed was not personal or emotional but political. Poverty, crime, sexism, and racism often feature heavily, and many stories display the moral decay of the planter aristocracy.

Probably the most significant Southern gothic novel is William Faulkner's *The Sound and the Fury*, which tells the story of a formerly aristocratic Southern family at the beginning of the twentieth century. In Faulkner's hands, the postwar Southern aristocratic family is abusive, sexually stunted and repressed, incestuous, and psychologically unstable. Faulkner's Southern gothic focussed on the deteriorating sanity and moral corruption necessary to exist in the South.

The Sir Walter Disease

The eminent satirist of the late nineteenth century, Mark Twain, had a unique take on what caused the Civil War. Eighteen years after it ended, in his book *Life on the Mississippi*, he took to task the famous English romantic novelist, Sir Walter Scott.

Then comes Sir Walter Scott with his enchantments, and by his single might... sets the world in love with dreams and phantoms; with decayed and swinish forms of religion; with *decayed and degraded systems of government*; with the sillinesses and emptinesses, sham grandeurs, sham gauds, and sham chivalries of a brainless and worthless long-vanished society. He did measureless harm; more real and lasting harm, perhaps, than any other individual that ever wrote… *It was Sir Walter that made every gentleman in the South a Major or a Colonel, or a General or a Judge, before the war; and it was he, also, that made these gentlemen value these bogus decorations.*

For it was he that created rank and caste down there, and also reverence for rank and caste, and pride and pleasure in them. Enough is laid on slavery, without fathering upon it these creations and contributions of Sir Walter… Sir Walter had so large a hand in making Southern character, as it existed before the war, that he is in great measure responsible for the war.

Twain might have been joking around, but he was also making an observant point. Compared to the rest of the United States or even western Europe during the mid-to-late nineteenth century, the American South was obsessed with inherited rank and name. That obsession with family status is what Faulkner skewers in *The Sound and the Fury*, and while blaming the entire Civil War on it is a simplification, it wasn't *not* a factor in the way it played out.

To Kill a Mockingbird

Just as well known in the Southern gothic genre as *The Sound and the Fury* (and a much easier read) is Harper Lee's *To Kill a Mockingbird*. There isn't much aristocracy in *To Kill a Mockingbird*, and the villains are not ex-planters but poor white Southerners who pitted themselves against black former slaves and their descendants. While *The Sound and the Fury* is mainly about class, *To Kill a Mockingbird* is mainly about race.

To Kill a Mockingbird shows how the justice system in the South is skewed against even the most moral and innocent black Southerners and how strongly prejudice persisted against them, even the better part of a century after the Civil War. Slavery might have ended, and many people would be content to consider the problem of racism "solved," but *To Kill a Mockingbird* shows how the unwritten laws of Southern communities can be deadly to the black people trying to exist in the South. Both the book and the film version are massively successful and are often read or shown in schools to discuss issues of race and tolerance.

Gone with the Wind

Not all well-known or significant books about the American South are scathing, gothic treatments. Many people's main impression of the South during the Civil War comes from the bestselling novel (and smash hit film) *Gone with the Wind*. This novel (and film) portray a highly romantic version of the South before the Civil War, through the eyes of a "southern belle" (a beautiful, rich, Southern woman) named Scarlett O'Hara. *Gone with the Wind* tells the story of how the spoiled Scarlett's life is changed by the Civil War, as her family's plantation is destroyed by Union soldiers.

It was published in 1936—hardly a great time for race relations in America—but even taking into account the publication date, *Gone with the Wind* has been criticized for portraying the South in an unnecessarily positive light. Scarlett is surrounded by slaves who are dedicated to her, and the novel and film have nothing much bad to say about slavery or the plantation system. A number of "house slaves" choose to stay "loyal" to Scarlett after they are freed, suggesting that life as a slave wasn't that bad. In fairness, it's well-documented that "house slaves" had far better lives than "field slaves" doing manual labor outdoors, but it was still a pretty miserable life in general.

Margaret Mitchell, the author, argued that slavery was not what the novel was about. She said it was instead about survival. However, history has placed *Gone with the Wind* in the genre of "anti-Tom literature," books that portrayed happy, docile slaves, in opposition to books like Harriet Beecher Stowe's

Uncle Tom's Cabin. Gone with the Wind even mentions *Uncle Tom's Cabin* disparagingly, saying that the North unquestioningly accepted it as "revelation second only to the Bible."

Despite the controversy, *Gone with the Wind* has sold over thirty million copies and remains one of the most recognizable pieces of American literature in history.

Django Unchained

Not every movie set in the prewar South is nearly as loving towards it as *Gone with the Wind*, but many of them face criticism for falling into the same traps and stereotypes that have made *Gone with the Wind* controversial. Quentin Tarantino's blood-soaked tribute to the Western genre, *Django Unchained*, is set in the South but has none of the gloss or "longing for times gone by" that characterizes *Gone with the Wind*. The main character is a former slave who partners with a bounty hunter and is the only significant slave character in the story who has any notable interest in escaping from slavery. Jesse Williams criticized Tarantino for portraying "plantations [that] are nearly empty farms with well-dressed Negresses in flowing gowns, frolicking on swings and enjoying leisurely strolls through the grounds, as if the setting is Versailles, mixed in with occasional acts of barbarism against slaves."

Films about Lincoln

Abraham Lincoln is probably the most popular subject for films *about* the Civil War, if we take away ones that just happen to take place *during* the Civil War and are more about life for people outside politics (like *Gone with the Wind*), and films that take place *after* the Civil War and deal with the fallout (like *To Kill a Mockingbird*). Lincoln has undoubtedly become one of the most celebrated American icons, from his instantly recognizable appearance to his reputation for honesty. His tragic death has also made a strong backdrop for political thrillers and character-driven costume dramas alike.

The 2010s alone saw the release of four Lincoln movies: *Killing Lincoln*, a National Geographic film released in 2013 dramatizing the plot to assassinate Lincoln; *Saving Lincoln*, also in 2013, which was a biographical film about Lincoln's bodyguard; *Lincoln*, directed by Steven Spielberg and starring Daniel Day-Lewis in 2012; and, of course, the famous *Abraham Lincoln: Vampire Hunter* in 2012, which dramatized the apparent secret life of Abraham Lincoln as a vampire hunter.

Glory

When you have big names and personalities like Abraham Lincoln to make movies about, sometimes it's easy to forget that the majority of people affected by the Civil War were just normal, everyday civilians who had their own reasons for getting involved in the fighting. The 1989 film *Glory* is about the first African-American regiment on the Union side of the Civil War.

Glory was based on letters written by Colonel Robert Gould Shaw, who was the son of abolitionists and commanded the 54th Massachusetts regiment, the first one in the Civil War to be made up of black soldiers. The 54th Massachusetts regiment campaigned to be paid equally to white troops, and the unit's prominence inspired many more black Americans to join the Union army and fight for their rights.

The film stars Denzel Washington and Morgan Freeman, and was the first major film about the role of black soldiers in the Civil War.

Civil War Board Games

Lest you think that the Civil War is confined to thoughtful, grim films and books that deconstruct Southern morality and seriously portray the tragedies of history, let us not forget that between 1961 and 2010, no fewer than twenty board games were created based on the Civil War.

Battle-Cry, released in 1961, is the best-selling Civil War game and involves capturing railroads to navigate over a map. It came with a thirty-one-page booklet summarizing the history of the Civil War, theoretically so that players could recreate real war tactics while they were trying to capture the railroads.

War Between the States, released in the late 1970s, has three enormous maps, 1,400 playing pieces, and demands that players take turns carrying out multiple different types of tasks, including producing supplies, building blockades, and navigating political alliances. It can easily take days to play and comes with a twenty-page rulebook.

Some games which require Confederate players have been criticised for buying into the "lost cause of the Confederacy" myth. Critics argue that these games unnecessarily deify the South or eliminate any reason for a player thinking that the South might be "worse" than the North. Probably unsurprisingly, not many of these big epic games have much to say about the causes of the war.

The American Oracle

Author and historian Robert Penn Warren described the American Civil War as the "American Oracle," and made the argument that the way the United States respond to the war is a litmus test for American cultural values.

For example, in 1913, both Union and Confederate veterans were invited to a ceremony commemorating the fiftieth anniversary of the Battle of Gettysburg. It was meant to be a show of brotherhood and reconciliation. But black veterans were excluded from the ceremony.

During the civil rights struggles of the 1950s and 1960s, when race was an especially touchy issue and the people in power had a vested interest in trying to downplay American racism, school textbooks glossed over the fact that the Civil War was mostly about the right to own slaves. They talked about "states' rights" but conveniently skipped mentioning what those rights were supposed to be.

Warren's book was published in 1961, so he can't exactly speak to 2018's political situation, but a look at the headlines today would certainly convince him that the American public hasn't forgotten the war and has a whole new set of reactions to it compared to the ones in the sixties.

The Confederate Flag

In 2016 and 2017, the issue of the Confederate flag became a hot-button discussion topic. Should it be legal to display the Confederate flag, or is it a hate symbol?

On the one hand, there's no denying that the Confederate flag was designed specifically for an army that wanted to enforce racially-based slavery.

Anyone who says otherwise just doesn't know the historical facts. That makes a pretty good case for banning it, in the same way that the swastika was banned in Germany after the Nazis used it as the symbol for their anti-Jewish regime.

On the other hand, many supporters of the Confederate flag today argue that calling it an anti-black symbol simplifies the issues of the Civil War. They claim that they're *obviously* not supporting slavery in 2017, so why can't they use the flag to represent states' rights or the other issues of the war?

Besides that, there's the whole question of free speech, which is protected by the American constitution in ways that other free speech laws aren't. The American constitution has been notoriously lenient about what free speech laws protect. Other countries, such as Germany or even Canada, are stricter about what counts as "speech that incites hatred or violence" (and thus isn't protected). So, does a government have any right to ban a Confederate flag at all unless it's accompanied by someone actually *saying* that we should have slavery again?

This book certainly doesn't have any answers, but hopefully it has given you a bit more of the context necessary for you to draw your own conclusions about this controversial issue.

Morality in Politics

There's a reason that the United States Constitution (and many other modern democracies) mandated a separation between Church and State, and it wasn't just to protect members of religious minorities. The entire purpose of democracy is to find a compromise or common ground. It demands conversation, seeing your opponent's side, and finding a solution that you can both agree on.

As soon as religion enters the mix, compromise goes out the window. No one wants to compromise on morality. No one wants to find common ground with someone they consider evil.

See where I'm going with this? The argument about slavery that was central to the Civil War got turned into a *moral* issue, not an economic one. Remember John C. Calhoun's speech about slavery as a "positive good"? Remember how abolitionists focussed on the innate sinfulness of owning slaves? It doesn't matter how justified that moral stance was, it meant that it was impossible for the two sides to have a conversation about it because both sides were morally convinced that they were right.

So, here's something to keep in mind next time you want to pull out morality in a political argument: you're probably not going to convince your opponent to change their moral system. What you probably *will* do is get them to dig their heels in and resist you with all their might. Even if at the end of the debate you feel like you've "won," you might just have made an embittered, long-term enemy like Northern abolitionists made of Southern Democrats.

RANDOM FACTS

1. One big political truism that the Civil War cemented in the American political system was that federal law overrode state law. This has led to a lot of modern controversy about what kind of laws the federal government is allowed to pass, but basically, if it's in the constitution, no state can pass a state law against it.

2. In 2009, the Museum of the Confederacy in Richmond, Virginia, was visited by a woman who claimed that her Confederate ancestor had conveyed secret messages around the South using a small, acorn-shaped device that he hid inside his rectum. However, she did not donate it to the museum and her claim has not been substantiated.

3. The Civil War was the first war to use an ambulance corps and battlefield hospitals. After the war, the nurses and doctors went on to write about their experiences and contributed hugely to modern medical advances, from anesthesia to antiseptics. Their experiences and writings saved millions of lives in World War One and World War Two.

4. The amendments protecting the right to vote for

black men encouraged many women to pursue their right to vote. If all Americans were supposed to have all the rights of citizens— including and *especially* the right to vote—then why was it still being denied to women? The female suffrage movement (the movement for women's voting rights) gained enormous momentum after the Civil War.

5. Yes, there was an element of racism to the female suffrage movement, something like, "what do you mean you're letting *black* men vote before you let *white* women vote?" The majority of female suffragists weren't especially interested in getting voting rights extended to black women.

6. Publishers estimate that about 60,000 books about the American Civil War have been published with more coming out all the time. It's an extremely popular setting for historical fiction and a hot topic for non-fiction history books (like this one).

7. There are also over a hundred films about or set in the Civil War and Reconstruction period, not even counting the innumerable made-for-TV documentaries on the subject.

8. *Captain America: Civil War* borrowed the name of the war to describe the breakdown of the central character, Captain America, as well as his group

of fellow superheroes. The film version is Marvel's fourth-highest grossing film yet (out of around fifty).

9. Abraham Lincoln was nicknamed "Honest Abe" long before he became president. However, if you've heard the anecdote about him cutting down a cherry tree as a child and refusing to lie about it to his father... well, first, that story's supposed to be about George Washington, and second, it definitely didn't happen, even to Washington. Not so honest after all!

10. Abraham Lincoln was the only American president to have a patent on an invention.

11. He was also responsible for getting a telegraph installed at the White House.

12. Speaking of inventions, the Civil War popularized many modern everyday items, like can openers, differently-shaped left and right shoes, and standardized clothing sizing.

13. Jim Crow laws were so good at segregating white and black people that the South African government used them as inspiration when they were developing their own laws about segregation for apartheid in the 1940s and 1950s.

14. Thomas D. Rice, the actor who wrote and performed the song "Jump Jim Crow" mostly

portrayed his character in the stereotypical and pretty offensive way that blackface performances usually portrayed black people. However, in 1832, he wrote some extra verses to the "Jump Jim Crow" song, opposing slavery and promoting solidarity by saying:

Should they get to fighting, perhaps the blacks will rise,

For their wish for freedom is shining in their eyes...

I'm for freedom and for Union altogether

Although I'm a black man, the white is called my brother.

15. William Faulkner, the author of *The Sound and the Fury*, criticised Southern "Civil War nostalgia" even more explicitly in his novel *Intruder in the Dust* when he said that "for every Southern boy fourteen years old, there is an instant when it's still not yet two o'clock on that July afternoon [when Robert E. Lee was defeated]".

16. The film version of *To Kill a Mockingbird* is just as well-known as the book for its treatment of social issues regarding race in the South. According to his biographer Neal Gabler, Walt Disney said, "that's the kind of film I wish I could make" after he saw the movie.

17. *To Kill a Mockingbird* remains one of the most often banned books in American schools for reasons ranging from the fact that it uses racial slurs (no matter how negatively it portrays the people who say them) to its core court case being about rape, to it, quote, "making people uncomfortable" as a 2017 Mississippi school district complained.

18. The first national cemetery in America was built for veterans of the Civil War.

19. The enormous numbers of widows and orphans left behind by the Civil War also prompted the first social care programs for veterans' families.

20. Mark Twain probably summed up the overwhelming effect of the Civil War on American culture best when he quotes a Southern gentleman in *Life on the Mississippi*: "In the war, each of us, in his own person, seems to have sampled all the different varieties of human experience; as a consequence, you can't mention an outside matter of any sort but it will certainly remind some listener of something that happened during the war—and out he comes with it. Of course, that brings the talk back to the war."

Test Yourself – Questions and Answers

1. How many board games based on the Civil War were created between 1961 and 2010?

   a. 4
   b. 20
   c. 50

2. Which of the following was not a Civil War innovation?

   a. Can openers
   b. A telegraph line to the White House
   c. The tank

3. What was the significance of George Gautier's book *Harder than Death*?

   a. It was the first major modern description of post-traumatic stress disorder
   b. It was written by the Civil War soldier with the highest body count
   c. It was written by the last surviving Civil War soldier

4. Which of these books is not in the Southern gothic genre?

   a. *The Sound and the Fury* by William Faulkner
   b. *To Kill a Mockingbird* by Harper Lee
   c. *Gone with the Wind* by Margaret Mitchell

5. What does Mark Twain blame the Civil War on?

    a. Slavery
    b. A debate over states' rights
    c. Sir Walter Scott's hyper-romantic ideas about class and rank.

Answers

1. b
2. c
3. a
4. c
5. c

MORE BOOKS BY BILL O'NEILL

I hope you enjoyed this book and learned something new. Please feel free to check out some of my previous books.

Made in the USA
Las Vegas, NV
13 April 2021

21340741R00094